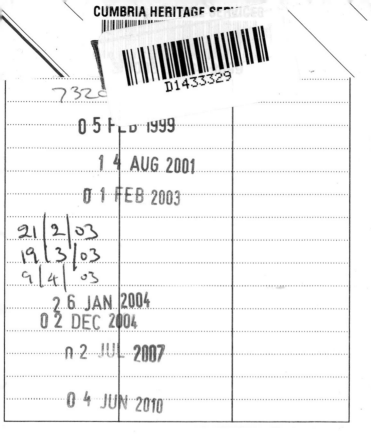

EVERYMAN'S LIBRARY
POCKET POETS

POEMS OF
··············
MOURNING

SELECTED AND
EDITED BY
PETER WASHINGTON

EVERYMAN'S LIBRARY
POCKET POETS

This selection by Peter Washington first published in
Everyman's Library, 1998

© David Campbell Publishers Ltd., 1998

A list of acknowledgments to copyright owners can be found at the back of
this volume.

ISBN 1-85715-736-2

A CIP catalogue record for this book is available from the British Library

Published by David Campbell Publishers Ltd.,
79 Berwick Street, London W1V 3PF

Distributed by Random House (UK) Ltd.,
20 Vauxhall Bridge Road, London SW1V 2SA

Typography by Peter B. Willberg

Typeset by AccComputing, Castle Cary, Somerset

Printed and bound in Germany
by Graphischer Großbetrieb Pößneck GmbH

CONTENTS

10

11

FOREWORD

Many cultures identify mourning as the very source
of poetry and music, what Elizabeth Bishop calls the
art of losing. That might well be the title of this
collection. Not every poem is concerned with death
but all are about loss.

Broadly speaking, my sequence moves from the
general to the particular. The relationship within each
poem between public voice and personal feeling is a
complex matter, too difficult to categorize in a short
book. For that reason I have refrained from dividing
the anthology into sections.

Nevertheless, all the major verse forms of mourning
are represented here: epitaph, requiem and lament.
Four great elegies by Milton, Gray, Whitman and
Rilke are surrounded by a wide variety of shorter
poems. Naturally, the pathos of death predominates,
but its comedy has not been neglected, whether in the
savage poems of World War I or the gentle teasing of
seventeenth-century satire.

PETER WASHINGTON

THE SONGS I HAD

The songs I had are withered
Or vanished clean,
Yet there are bright tracks
Where I have been,

And there grow flowers
For others' delight.
Think well, O singer,
Soon comes night.

INTO MY HEART AN AIR
THAT KILLS
From *A Shropshire Lad*

Into my heart an air that kills
    From yon far country blows:
What are those blue remembered hills,
    What spires, what farms are those?

That is the land of lost content,
    I see it shining plain,
The happy highways where I went
    And cannot come again.

IN MEMORIAM (XI)

Calm is the morn without a sound,
    Calm as to suit a calmer grief,
    And only thro' the faded leaf
The chestnut pattering to the ground:

Calm and deep peace on this high wold,
    And on these dews that drench the furze,
    And all the silvery gossamers
That twinkle into green and gold:

Calm and still light on yon great plain
    That sweeps with all its autumn bowers,
    And crowded farms and lessening towers,
To mingle with the bounding main:

Calm and deep peace in this wide air,
    These leaves that redden to the fall;
    And in my heart, if calm at all,
If any calm, a calm despair:

Calm on the seas, and silver sleep,
    And waves that sway themselves in rest,
    And dead calm in that noble breast
Which heaves but with the heaving deep.

ALFRED, LORD TENNYSON

WHAT SURVIVES

Who says that all must vanish?
Who knows, perhaps the flight
of the bird you wound remains,
and perhaps flowers survive
caresses in us, in their ground.

It isn't the gesture that lasts,
but it dresses you again in gold
armor – from breast to knees –
and the battle was so pure
an Angel wears it after you.

RAINER MARIA RILKE
TRANS. A. POULIN

WHEN I HAVE FEARS

When I have fears that I may cease to be
Before my pen has glean'd my teeming brain,
Before high-pilèd books, in charact'ry,
Hold like rich garners the full-ripen'd grain;
When I behold, upon the night's starr'd face,
Huge cloudy symbols of a high romance,
And feel that I may never live to trace
Their shadows, with the magic hand of chance;
And when I feel, fair creature of an hour!
That I shall never look upon thee more,
Never have relish in the faery power
Of unreflecting love: – then on the shore
    Of the wide world I stand alone, and think,
    Till Love and Fame to nothingness do sink.

BECAUSE THAT YOU ARE GOING

Because that you are going
And never coming back
And I, however absolute,
May overlook your Track –

Because that Death is final,
However first it be,
This instant be suspended
Above Mortality –

Significance that each has lived
The other to detect
Discovery not God himself
Could now annihilate

Eternity, Presumption
The instant I perceive
That you, who were Existence
Yourself forgot to live –

The 'Life that is' will then have been
A thing I never knew –
As Paradise fictitious
Until the Realm of you –

The 'Life that is to be,' to me,
A Residence too plain
Unless in my Redeemer's Face
I recognize your own –

Of Immortality who doubts
He may exchange with me
Curtailed by your obscuring Face
Of everything but He –

Of Heaven and Hell I also yield
The Right to reprehend
To whoso would commute this Face
For his less priceless Friend.

If 'God is Love' as he admits
We think that he must be
Because he is a 'jealous God'
He tells us certainly

If 'All is possible with' him
As he besides concedes
He will refund us finally
Our confiscated Gods –

A DIRGE, FROM *THE WHITE DIVEL*

Call for the Robin-Red-Brest and the Wren,
Since ore shadie groues they houer,
And with leaues and flowres do couer
The friendlesse bodies of unburied men.
Call unto his funerall Dole
The Ante, the field-mouse, and the mole
To reare him hillockes, that shall keep him warme,
And (when gay tombes are rob'd) sustaine no harme,
But keepe the wolfe far thence: that's foe to men,
For with his nailes hee'l dig them up agen.

IN MEMORIAM (II)

Old Yew, which graspest at the stones
   That name the under-lying dead,
   Thy fibres net the dreamless head,
Thy roots are wrapt about the bones.

The seasons bring the flower again,
   And bring the firstling to the flock;
   And in the dusk of thee, the clock
Beats out the little lives of men.

O not for thee the glow, the bloom,
   Who changest not in any gale,
   Nor branding summer suns avail
To touch thy thousand years of gloom:

And gazing on thee, sullen tree,
   Sick for thy stubborn hardihood,
   I seem to fail from out my blood
And grow incorporate into thee.

FUTILITY

Move him into the sun –
Gently its touch awoke him once,
At home, whispering of fields half-sown.
Always it woke him, even in France,
Until this morning and this snow.
If anything might rouse him now
The kind old sun will know.

Think how it wakes the seeds –
Woke once the clays of a cold star.
Are limbs, so dear achieved, are sides
Full-nerved, still warm, too hard to stir?
Was it for this the clay grew tall?
– O what made fatuous sunbeams toil
To break earth's sleep at all?

I HEARD A FLY BUZZ

I heard a Fly buzz – when I died –
The Stillness in the Room
Was like the Stillness in the Air –
Between the Heaves of Storm –

The Eyes around – had wrung them dry –
And Breaths were gathering firm
For that last Onset – when the King
Be witnessed – in the Room –

I willed my Keepsakes – Signed away
What portion of me be
Assignable – and then it was
There interposed a Fly –

With Blue – uncertain stumbling Buzz –
Between the light – and me –
And then the Windows failed – and then
I could not see to see –

THEN

Then when the ample season
Warmed us, waned and went,
We gave to the leaves no graves,
To the robin gone no name,
Nor thought at the birds' return
Of their sourceless dim descent,
And we read no loss in the leaf,
But a freshness ever the same.

The leaf first learned of years
One not forgotten fall;
Of lineage now, and loss
These latter singers tell,
Of a year when birds now still
Were all one choiring call
Till the unreturning leaves
Imperishably fell.

FAREWELL WITHOUT A GUITAR

Spring's bright paradise has come to this.
Now the thousand-leaved green falls to the ground.
Farewell, my days.

The thousand-leaved red
Comes to this thunder of light
As its autumnal terminal –

A Spanish storm,
A wide, still Aragonese,
In which the horse walks home without a rider,

Head down. The reflections and repetitions,
The blows and buffets of fresh senses
Of the rider that was,

Are a final construction,
Like glass and sun, of male reality
And of that other and her desire.

DIRGE FOR FIDELE
From *Cymbeline*, IV ii

Fear no more the heat o' the sun,
　　Nor the furious winter's rages;
Thou thy worldly task hast done,
　　Home art gone, and ta'en thy wages;
Golden lads and girls all must
　　As chimney-sweepers, come to dust.

Fear no more the frown o' the great,
　　Thou art past the tyrant's stroke:
Care no more to clothe and eat;
　　To thee the reed is as the oak;
The sceptre, learning, physic, must
　　All follow this, and come to dust.

Fear no more the lightning-flash,
　　Nor the all-dreaded thunder-stone;
Fear not slander, censure rash;
　　Thou hast finish'd joy and moan;
All lovers young, all lovers must
　　Consign to thee, and come to dust.

No exorciser harm thee!
    Nor no witchcraft charm thee!
Ghost unlaid forbear thee!
    Nothing ill come near thee!
Quiet consummation have;
    And renownèd be thy grave!

SPRING AND FALL:
to a young child

Márgarét, áre you gríeving
Over Goldengrove unleaving?
Leáves, líke the things of man, you
With your fresh thoughts care for, can you?
Áh! ás the heart grows older
It will come to such sights colder
By and by, nor spare a sigh
Though worlds of wanwood leafmeal lie;
And yet you *will* weep and know why.
Now no matter, child, the name:
Sórrow's spríngs áre the same.
Nor mouth had, no nor mind, expressed
What heart heard of, ghost guessed:
It ís the blight man was born for,
It is Margaret you mourn for.

BLACK SPRING

A half-holiday for the burial. Of course, they punish
the provincial copper bells for hours;
terribly the nose tilts up like a tallow candle
from the coffin. Does it wish to draw breath
from its torso in a mourning suit? The last snow
fell sombrely – white, then the roads were bread-
      crumbed with pebbles.
Poor winter, honeycombed with debts,
poured to corruption. Now the dumb, black springtime
must look into the chilly eye ... from under the mould
on the roof-shingles, the liquid oatmeal
of the roads, the green stubble of life
on our faces! High in the splinter elm,
shrill the annual fledglings with their spikey necks.
They say to man that his road is mud,
his luck is rutted – there is nothing
sorrier than the marriage of two deaths.

ANAPHORA
In memory of Marjorie Carr Stevens

Each day with so much ceremony
begins, with birds, with bells,
with whistles from a factory;
such white-gold skies our eyes
first open on, such brilliant walls
that for a moment we wonder
'Where is the music coming from, the energy?
The day was meant for what ineffable creature
we must have missed?' Oh promptly he
appears and takes his earthly nature
   instantly, instantly falls
   victim of long intrigue,
   assuming memory and mortal
   mortal fatigue.

More slowly falling into sight
and showering into stippled faces,
darkening, condensing all his light;
in spite of all the dreaming
squandered upon him with that look,
suffers our uses and abuses,
sinks through the drift of bodies,
sinks through the drift of classes
to evening to the beggar in the park

who, weary, without lamp or book
    prepares stupendous studies:
    the fiery event
    of every day in endless
    endless assent.

THAT IT WILL NEVER COME AGAIN

That it will never come again
Is what makes life so sweet.
Believing what we don't believe
Does not exhilarate.

That if it be, it be at best
An ablative estate –
This instigates an appetite
Precisely opposite.

FOR WHOM THE BELL TOLLS

Aircrews have had it and the war goes on
And I have had it if I die to-morrow,
Not needing the marvellous conceits of Donne
Or any word of fear or sound of sorrow.
Love I have had, the climax of all lives,
Traditionally the enemy of death,
That like an Old Testament prophet power-dives
And takes away the hard-drawn, precious breath.

Yeats read much in old poets all his life
And prophecies and dreams of golden sages,
Condensed past wisdom into a few pages,
But in his passionate intellectual strife
Had not the art new generations praise,
To cram a lifetime into seven days.

THE GHOST

'Who knocks?' 'I, who was beautiful,
　　Beyond all dreams to restore,
I, from the roots of the dark thorn am hither.
　　And knock on the door.'

'Who speaks?' 'I – once was my speech
　　Sweet as the bird's on the air,
When echo lurks by the waters to heed;
　　'Tis I speak thee fair.'

'Dark is the hour!' 'Ay, and cold.'
　　'Lone is my house.' 'Ah, but mine?'
'Sight, touch, lips, eyes yearned in vain.'
　　'Long dead these to thine . . .'

Silence. Still faint on the porch
　　Brake the flames of the stars.
In gloom groped a hope-wearied hand
　　Over keys, bolts, and bars.

A face peered. All the grey night
　　In chaos of vacancy shone;
Nought but vast sorrow was there –
　　The sweet cheat gone.

THE GLIMPSE

She sped through the door
And, following in haste,
And stirred to the core,
I entered hot-faced;
But I could not find her,
No sign was behind her.
'Where is she?' I said:
– 'Who?' they asked that sat there;
'Not a soul's come in sight.'
– 'A maid with red hair.'
– 'Ah.' They paled. 'She is dead.
People see her at night,
But you are the first
On whom she has burst
In the keen common light.'

It was ages ago,
When I was quite strong:
I have waited since, – O,
I have waited so long!
– Yea, I set me to own
The house, where now lone
I dwell in void rooms
Booming hollow as tombs!
But I never come near her,

Though nightly I hear her.
And my cheek has grown thin
And my hair has grown gray
With this waiting therein;
But she still keeps away!

ROMAN SARCOPHAGI

Why should we too, though, not anticipate
(set down here and assigned our places thus)
that only for a short time rage and hate
and this bewildering will remain in us,

as in the ornate sarcophagus, enclosed
with images of gods, rings, glasses, trappings,
there lay in slowly self-consuming wrappings
something being slowly decomposed –

till swallowed by those unknown mouths at last,
that never speak. (Where bides a brain that may
yet trust the utterance of its thinking to them?)

Then from the ancient aqueducts there passed
eternal water into them one day: –
that mirrors now and moves and sparkles
   through them.

LAST LOVE

Love at the closing of our days
is apprehensive and very tender.
Glow brighter, brighter, farewell rays
of one last love in its evening splendour.

Blue shade takes half the world away:
through western clouds alone some light is slanted.
O tarry, O tarry, declining day,
enchantment, let me stay enchanted.

The blood runs thinner, yet the heart
remains as ever deep and tender.
O last belated love, thou art
a blend of joy and of hopeless surrender.

FROM FAR, FROM EVE
AND MORNING
From *A Shropshire Lad*

From far, from eve and morning
   And yon twelve-winded sky,
The stuff of life to knit me
   Blew hither: here am I.

Now – for a breath I tarry
   Nor yet disperse apart –
Take my hand quick and tell me,
   What have you in your heart.

Speak now, and I will answer;
   How shall I help you, say;
Ere to the wind's twelve quarters
   I take my endless way.

ODES III, 30: *Exegi Monumentum*

'No hands have wrought my monument; no weeds
will hide the nation's footpath to its site.
Tsar Alexander's column it exceeds
   in splendid insubmissive height.

'Not all of me is dust. Within my song,
safe from the worm, my spirit will survive,
and my sublunar frame will dwell as long
   as there is one last bard alive.

'Throughout great Rus' my echoes will extend,
and all will name me, all tongues in her use:
the Slavs' proud heir, the Finn, the Kalmuk, friend
   of steppes, the yet untamed Tunguz.

'And to the people long shall I be dear
because kind feelings did my lyre extoll,
invoking freedom in an age of fear,
   and mercy for the broken soul.'

Obey thy God, and never mind, O Muse,
the laurels or the stings: make it thy rule
to be unstirred by praise as by abuse,
   and do not contradict the fool.

TRANS. ALEXANDER PUSHKIN AND
VLADIMIR NABOKOV

ALL BUT DEATH, CAN BE ADJUSTED

All but Death, can be Adjusted –
Dynasties repaired –
Systems – settled in their Sockets –
Citadels – dissolved –

Wastes of Lives – resown with Colors
By Succeeding Springs –
Death – unto itself – Exception –
Is exempt from Change –

REMEMBER

Remember me when I am gone away,
   Gone far away into the silent land;
   When you can no more hold me by the hand,
Nor I half turn to go yet turning stay.
Remember me when no more day by day
   You tell me of our future that you planned:
   Only remember me; you understand
It will be late to counsel then or pray.
Yet if you should forget me for a while
   And afterwards remember, do not grieve:
   For if the darkness and corruption leave
   A vestige of the thoughts that once I had,
Better by far you should forget and smile
   Than that you should remember and be sad.

SIMPLIFY ME WHEN I'M DEAD

Remember me when I am dead
and simplify me when I'm dead.

As the processes of earth
strip off the colour and the skin:
take the brown hair and blue eye

and leave me simpler than at birth,
when hairless I came howling in
as the moon entered the cold sky.

Of my skeleton perhaps,
so stripped, a learned man will say
'He was of such a type and intelligence,' no more.

Thus when in a year collapse
particular memories, you may
deduce, from the long pain I bore

the opinions I held, who was my foe
and what I left, even my appearance
but incidents will be no guide.

Time's wrong-way telescope will show
a minute man ten years hence
and by distance simplified.

Through that lens see if I seem
substance or nothing: of the world
deserving mention or charitable oblivion,

not by momentary spleen
or love into decision hurled,
leisurely arrive at an opinion.

Remember me when I am dead
and simplify me when I'm dead.

AQUA MORTIS

Death's elixirs have their own golden gleam.
I see you clearly: one good, failing eye's
on morning piss caught clumsily 'midstream'
it's your first task of the day to analyse.

Each day dawns closer to the last *eureka*,
the urine phial held up to clouding rays
meaning all solutions in life's beaker
precipitate one night from all our days.

Alchemists keep skulls, and you have one
that stretches your skin taut and moulds your face,
and instead of a star sphere for sense of space
there's the transatlantic number of your son,
a 14-digit spell propped by the phone
whose girdling's giddy speed knocks spots off Puck's
but can't re-eye dry sockets or flesh bone.

My study is your skull. *I'll burn my books.*

DIED OF WOUNDS

His wet white face and miserable eyes
Brought nurses to him more than groans and sighs:
But hoarse and low and rapid rose and fell
His troubled voice: he did the business well.

The ward grew dark; but he was still complaining
And calling out for 'Dickie'. 'Curse the Wood!
'It's time to go. O Christ, and what's the good?
'We'll never take it, and it's always raining.'

I wondered where he'd been; then heard him shout,
'They snipe like hell! O Dickie, don't go out' . . .
I fell asleep . . . Next morning he was dead;
And some Slight Wound lay smiling on the bed.

POOR TOM

Here, a sheer hulk, lies poor Tom Bowling,
    The darling of our crew,
No more he'll hear the tempest howling,
    For death has broach'd him to;

His form was of the manliest beauty,
    His heart was kind and soft,
Faithful below he did his duty,
    But now he's gone aloft.

Tom never from his word departed,
    His virtues were so rare,
His friends were many, and true-hearted,
    His Poll was kind and fair:

And then he'd sing so blith and jolly,
    Ah many's the time and oft!
But mirth is turn'd to melancholy,
    For Tom is gone aloft.

Yet shall poor Tom find pleasant weather,
    When he, who all commands,
Shall give, to call life's crew together,
    The word to pipe all hands:

Thus death, who kings and tars dispatches,
   In vain Tom's life has doff'd,
For though his body's under hatches,
   His soul is gone aloft.

MUSIC

Music, when soft voices die,
Vibrates in the memory –
Odours, when sweet violets sicken,
Live within the sense they quicken.
Rose leaves, when the rose is dead,
Are heaped for the belovèd's bed;
And so thy thoughts, when thou art gone,
Love itself shall slumber on.

BECAUSE I COULD NOT STOP FOR DEATH

Because I could not stop for Death –
He kindly stopped for me –
The Carriage held but just Ourselves –
And Immortality.

We slowly drove – He knew no haste
And I had put away
My labor and my leisure too,
For His Civility –

We passed the School, where Children strove
At Recess – in the Ring –
We passed the Fields of Gazing Grain –
We passed the Setting Sun –

Or rather – He passed Us –
The Dews drew quivering and chill --
For only Gossamer, my Gown –
My Tippet – only Tulle –

We paused before a House that seemed
A Swelling of the Ground –
The Roof was scarcely visible –
The Cornice – in the Ground –

Since then – 'tis Centuries – and yet
Feels shorter than the Day
I first surmised the Horses' Heads
Were toward Eternity –

AN ISLAND CEMETERY

This graveyard with its umbrella pines
Is inferior in status to the vines
And, though new guests keep crowding in,
Must stay the size it's always been.

Where men are many, acres few,
The dead must be cultivated too,
Like seeds in any farmer's field
Are planted for the bones they yield.

It takes about eighteen months for one
To ripen into a skeleton,
To be washed, folded, packed in a small
Niche hollowed out of the cemetery wall.

Curiosity made me stop
While sextons were digging up a crop:
Bards have taken it too amiss
That Alexanders come to this.

Wherever our personalities go
(And, to tell the truth, we do not know),
The solid structures they leave behind
Are no discredit to our kind.

Mourners may miss, and they do, a face,
But at least they cannot detect a trace
Of those fish-like hungers, mammalian heats,
That kin our flesh to the coarser meats.

And who would be ashamed to own
To a patience that we share with stone,
This underlying thing in us
Which never at any time made a fuss?

Considering what our motives are,
We ought to thank our lucky star
That Love must ride to reach his ends
A mount which has no need of friends.

IN A DISUSED GRAVEYARD

The living come with grassy tread
To read the gravestones on the hill;
The graveyard draws the living still,
But never any more the dead.

The verses in it say and say:
'The ones who living come today
To read the stones and go away
Tomorrow dead will come to stay.'

So sure of death the marble's rhyme,
Yet can't help marking all the time
How no one dead will seem to come.
What is it men are shrinking from?

It would be easy to be clever
And tell the stones: Men hate to die
And have stopped dying now forever.
I think they would believe the lie.

BALLADE OF THE LADIES
OF TIME PAST

O tell me where, in lands or seas,
Flora, that Roman belle, has strayed,
Thais, or Archipiades,
Who put each other in the shade,
Or Echo who by bank and glade
Gave back the crying of the hound,
And whose sheer beauty could not fade.
But where shall last year's snow be found?

Where too is learned Héloïse,
For whom shorn Abélard was made
A tonsured monk upon his knees?
Such tribute his devotion paid.
And where's that queen who, having played
With Buridan, had him bagged and bound
To swim the Seine thus ill-arrayed?
But where shall last year's snow be found?

Queen Blanche the fair, whose voice could please
As does the siren's serenade,
Great Bertha, Beatrice, Alice – these,
And Arembourg whom Maine obeyed,
And Joan whom Burgundy betrayed
And England burned, and Heaven crowned:

Where are they, Mary, Sovereign Maid?
But where shall last year's snow be found?

Not next week, Prince, nor next decade,
Ask me these questions I propound.
I shall but say again, dismayed,
Ah, where shall last year's snow be found?

FOR A DEAD LADY

No more with overflowing light
Shall fill the eyes that now are faded,
Nor shall another's fringe with night
Their woman-hidden world as they did.
No more shall quiver down the days
The flowing wonder of her ways,
Whereof no language may requite
The shifting and the many-shaded.

The grace, divine, definitive,
Clings only as a faint forestalling;
The laugh that love could not forgive
Is hushed, and answers to no calling;
The forehead and the little ears
Have gone where Saturn keeps the years;
The breast where roses could not live
Has done with rising and with falling.

The beauty, shattered by the laws
That have creation in their keeping,
No longer trembles at applause,
Or over children that are sleeping;
And we who delve in beauty's lore
Know all that we have known before
Of what inexorable cause
Makes Time so vicious in his reaping.

EDWARD ARLINGTON ROBINSON   59

ONE OF THE DEAD

Paler, not quite so fair as in her life,
   She lies upon the bed, perfectly still;
   Her little hands clasped with a patient will
Upon her bosom, swelling without strife;
An honoured virgin, a most blameless wife.
   The roses lean upon the window sill,
   That she trained once; their sweets the hot air fill,
And make the death-apartment odour-rife.
Her meek white hands folded upon her breast,
   Her gentle eyes closed in the long last sleep,
She lieth down in her unbroken rest;
   Her kin, kneeling around, a vigil keep,
Venting their grief in low sobs unrepressed: –
   Friends, she but slumbers, wherefore do ye weep?

TO PRAISE A DEAD WOMAN

Is it possible to praise a dead woman?
She is estranged and powerful ...
An alien-loving power has brought her
to a violent, hot grave.

The rigid swallows of her curved brows
flew to me from the grave
to say they had laid down to rest
in their cold Stockholm bed.

Your family were proud of your
        great-grandfather's violin,
and it was beautiful at the neck.
You parted your scarlet lips
in laughter, so Italian, so Russian.

I cherish your unhappy memory,
wilding, bear cub, Mignon.
But the wheels of the windmills hibernate in the snow,
and the postman's horn is frozen.

A YOUNG DEAD WOMAN

No matter who you are, you are alive: pass quickly
    Among the grasses by my humble vault:
    Don't crush the flowers where I lie unconsoled
    Listening to the climbing ant and ivy.

I think you stopped. That singing was a dove:
      it moaned.
    Oh no, don't sacrifice it on my tomb.
    To earn my favour, give it flight and freedom.
    Life is so sweet: oh, let it live, my friend.

    It was under the myrtle garland, at the door,
    On the sill of marriage I died, a virgin wife,
So near – already far from him I used to love.

    So my eyes closed against the happy light.
    And now I stay – alas, for evermore –
With Erebus deaf to prayers, in the embrace of Night.

JOSÉ-MARIA DE HEREDIA
    TRANS. ALISTAIR ELLIOT

EPITAPH

Oh you, passing by this hill – one
Among many – who mark this no longer solitary snow,
Hear my story. Stop for a few moments
Here where, dry-eyed, my comrades buried me,
Where, every summer, the gentle field-grass fed by me
Grows thicker and greener than elsewhere.
Killed by my companions for no small crime,
I, Micca the partisan, haven't lain here many years,
Hadn't lived many more when darkness struck.

Passer-by, I ask no pardon of you or any other,
No prayer or lament, no special remembrance.
Only one thing I beg: that this peace of mine endure,
That heat and cold succeed each other endlessly
    above me,
Without fresh blood filtering through clods
To reach me with its deadly warmth,
Waking to new pain these bones long turned to stone.

RAIN ON A GRAVE

Clouds spout upon her
    Their waters amain
    In ruthless disdain, –
Her who but lately
    Had shivered with pain
As at touch of dishonour
If there had lit on her
So coldly, so straightly
    Such arrows of rain:

One who to shelter
    Her delicate head
Would quicken and quicken
    Each tentative tread
If drops chanced to pelt her
    That summertime spills
    In dust-paven rills
When thunder-clouds thicken
    And birds close their bills.

Would that I lay there
    And she were housed here!
Or better, together
Were folded away there
Exposed to one weather

We both, – who would stray there
When sunny the day there,
   Or evening was clear
   At the prime of the year.

Soon will be growing
   Green blades from her mound,
And daisies be showing
   Like stars on the ground,
Till she form part of them –
Ay – the sweet heart of them,
   Loved beyond measure
   With a child's pleasure
   All her life's round.

IN MEMORIAM (VII)

Dark house, by which once more I stand
   Here in the long unlovely street,
   Doors, where my heart was used to beat
So quickly, waiting for a hand,

A hand that can be clasp'd no more –
   Behold me, for I cannot sleep,
   And like a guilty thing I creep
At earliest morning to the door.

He is not here; but far away
   The noise of life begins again,
   And ghastly thro' the drizzling rain
On the bald street breaks the blank day.

SHE DWELT AMONG THE UNTRODDEN WAYS

She dwelt among the untrodden ways
    Beside the springs of Dove,
A Maid whom there were none to praise
    And very few to love:

A violet by a mossy stone
    Half hidden from the eye!
– Fair as a star, when only one
    Is shining in the sky.

She lived unknown, and few could know
    When Lucy ceased to be;
But she is in her grave, and, oh,
    The difference to me!

THE SOUL DRIVEN FROM THE BODY

The soul driven from the body
Mourns the memory it leaves behind.

A dove hit in flight sadly turns
Its neck and sees its nest destroyed.

ABU AL-ALA AL-MA'ARRI
TRANS. G. B. H. WIGHTMAN AND
A. Y. AL-UDHARI

From HORACE, ODES II, 14
His age, Dedicated to his peculiar friend,
M. John Wickes, under the name of Posthumus

Ah Posthumus! Our yeares hence flye,
And leave no sound; nor piety,
     Or prayers, or vow
Can keepe the wrinkle from the brow:
     But we must on,
As Fate do's lead or draw us; none,
None, Posthumus, co'd ere decline
The doome of cruell Proserpine.

The pleasing wife, the house, the ground
Must all be left, no one plant found
     To follow thee,
Save only the Curst-Cipresse tree:
     A merry mind
Looks forward, scornes what's left behind:
Let's live, my Wickes, then, while we may,
And here enjoy our Holiday.

W'ave seen the past-best Times, and these
Will nere return, we see the Seas,
     And Moons to wain;
But they fill up their Ebbs again:
     But vanisht man,

Like to a Lilly-lost, nere can,
Nere can repullulate, or bring
His dayes to see a second Spring.

But on we must, and thither tend,
Where Anchus and rich Tullus blend
         Their sacred seed:
Thus has Infernall Jove decreed;
         We must be made,
Ere long, a song, ere long, a shade.
Why then, since life to us is short,
Lets make it full up, by our sport.

Crown we our Heads with Roses then,
And 'noint with Tirian Balme; for when
         We two are dead,
The world with us is buried.
         Then live we free,
As is the Air, and let us be
Our own fair wind, and mark each one
Day with the white and Luckie stone.

SONG

Oh the sad Day,
When friends shall shake their heads and say
Of miserable me,
Hark how he groans, look how he pants for breath,
See how he struggles with the pangs of Death!
When they shall say of these poor eyes,
How Hollow, and how dim they be!
Mark how his breast does swell and rise,
Against his potent enemy!
When some old Friend shall step to my Bed-side,
Touch my chill face, and thence shall gently slide,
And when his next companions say,
How does he do? what hopes? shall turn away,
Answering only with a lift up hand,
Who can his fate withstand?
Then shall a gasp or two, do more
Than e're my Rhetorick could before,
Perswade the peevish World to trouble me no more!

THOMAS FLATMAN

NEEDLES HAVE STITCHED
A DEATH SHROUD

Needles have stitched a death shroud with our life
    thread;
It caps our temples. The searching intellect

Sees light as newly created and darkness
As the dimension from which it was born.

Don't pray for a kingdom in case you try
To seize power with force. Kings are sad creatures.

Each sunset warns quiet men who look ahead
That light will end; and each day postman Death

Knocks on our door. Although he does not speak,
He hands us a standing invitation.

Be like those skeleton horses which scent battle
And fear to eat. They wait chewing their bridles.

72   ABU AL-ALA AL-MA'ARRI
      TRANS. G. B. H. WIGHTMAN AND
      A. Y. AL-UDHARI

SENECA'S TROAS, ACT 2

CHORUS

    After Death, nothing is, and Nothing, Death,
    The utmost Limit of a Gasp of Breath:
    Let the ambitious Zealot lay aside,
His hopes of Heav'n (whose Faith is but his Pride)
    Let Slavish Souls lay by their Fear,
    Nor be concern'd, which way, or where
    After this life they shall be hurl'd;
Dead, we become the Lumber of the World;
And to that Mass of Matter shall be swept,
Where things Destroy'd, with things Unborn are kept.
    Devouring time swallows us whole,
Impartial Death confounds Body and Soul.
    For Hell, and the foul Fiend that rules
    God's everlasting fiery Goales,
    Devis'd by Rogues, dreaded by Fools;
(With his grim griezly Dog, that keeps the Door)
    Are sensless Stories, idle Tales,
    Dreams, Whimseys, and no more.

WEEPING FOR THE
ZEN MASTER PO-YEN

Moss covers his stone bed fresh –
How many springs did the master occupy it?
They sketched preserve his form practicing
    the Way,
But burned away the body that sat in meditation.
The pagoda garden closes in snow on the pines,
While the library locks dust in the chinks.
I hate myself for these lines of tears falling –
I am not a man who understands the Void.

    TRANS. STEPHEN OWEN

WITH RUE MY HEART IS LADEN
From *A Shropshire Lad*

With rue my heart is laden
  For golden friends I had,
For many a rose-lipt maiden
  And many a lightfoot lad.

By brooks too broad for leaping
  The lightfoot boys are laid;
The rose-lipt girls are sleeping
  In fields where roses fade.

A. E. HOUSMAN   75

THE SUFI WHO THOUGHT HE HAD
LEFT THE WORLD

A sufi once, with nothing on his mind,
Was – without warning – struck at from behind.
He turned and murmured, choking back the tears:
'The man you hit's been dead for thirty years;
He's left this world!' The man who'd struck him said:
'You talk a lot for someone who is dead!
But talk's not action – while you boast, you stray
Further and further from the secret Way,
And while a hair of you remains, your heart
And Truth are still a hundred worlds apart.'
Burn all you have, all that you thought and knew
(Even your shroud must go; let that burn too),
Then leap into the flames, and as you burn
Your pride will falter, you'll begin to learn.
But keep one needle back and you will meet
A hundred thieves who force you to retreat
(Think of that tiny needle which became
The negligible cause of Jesus' shame).
As you approach this stage's final veil,
Kingdoms and wealth, substance and water fail;
Withdraw into yourself, and one by one
Give up the things you own – when this is done,

Be still in selflessness and pass beyond
All thoughts of good and evil; break this bond,
And as it shatters you are worthy of
Oblivion, the Nothingness of love.

FARID UD-DIN ATTAR   77
TRANS. AFKHAM DARBANDI AND DICK DAVIS

ONE ART

The art of losing isn't hard to master;
so many things seem filled with the intent
to be lost that their loss is no disaster.

Lose something every day. Accept the fluster
of lost door keys, the hour badly spent.
The art of losing isn't hard to master.

Then practice losing farther, losing faster:
places, and names, and where it was you meant
to travel. None of these will bring disaster.

I lost my mother's watch. And look! my last, or
next-to-last, of three loved houses went.
The art of losing isn't hard to master.

I lost two cities, lovely ones. And, vaster,
some realms I owned, two rivers, a continent.
I miss them, but it wasn't a disaster.

– Even losing you (the joking voice, a gesture
I love) I shan't have lied. It's evident
the art of losing's not too hard to master
though it may look like (*Write* it!) like disaster.

WRITING THE POEMS OF LOSS

Some poets even seem to enjoy
writing the poems of loss
that are so truly sad and affecting.
I've always preferred to keep hold,
loving the girl, though her loss
may be what I'm expecting.

A poem's no use on a bed
(though they talk of 'pleasing the eye');
its a poor, very poor, consolation.
What's the use, when she just isn't there,
bringing the tear to the eye
of Eng Lit admiration?

There's a time for the masterly plaint
weeping the loss of the flower.
That time isn't yet; so don't rush it.
Keep the heartfelt iambics on ice.
Human love is a delicate flower –
a canto could crush it.

TO LUIGI DEL RICCIO AFTER THE DEATH OF CECCHINO BRACCI

I scarcely knew him when his eyes were shut
For ever, he who was your life and light.
His eyes closed fast at death's last parting, but
Opened on God and found a love more bright.

I know and weep; yet it was not my fault
That I should meet him too late to admire
His grace. Your memory becomes his vault,
Lost not to you, only to my desire.

Then if, Luigi, I must carve the form
Of him, Cecchino, whom I speak about,
And change him from this dust to living stone,

You, his friend, must keep his image warm,
And if you fail, my art is called in doubt.
I'll find his likeness now in you alone.

SELVA OSCURA

A house can be haunted by those who were never there
If there was where they were missed. Returning
    to such
Is it worse if you miss the same another or none?
The haunting anyway is too much.
You have to leave the house to clear the air.

A life can be haunted by what it never was
If that were merely glimpsed. Lost in the maze
That means yourself and never out of the wood
These days, though lost, will be all your days;
Life, if you leave it, must be left for good.

And yet for good can be also where I am,
Stumbling among dark treetrunks, should I meet
One sudden shaft of light from the hidden sky
Or, finding bluebells bathe my feet,
Know that the world, though more, is also I.

Perhaps suddenly too I strike a clearing and see
Some unknown house – or was it mine? – but now
It welcomes whom I miss in welcoming me;
The door swings open and a hand
Beckons to all the life my days allow.

LOUIS MacNEICE

ELEGY FOR HIMSELF
Written in the Tower before his execution

My prime of youth is but a frost of cares;
  My feast of joy is but a dish of pain;
My crop of corn is but a field of tares;
  And all my good is but vain hope of gain:
The day is past, and yet I saw no sun;
And now I live, and now my life is done.

My tale was heard, and yet it was not told;
  My fruit is fall'n, and yet my leaves are green;
My youth is spent, and yet I am not old;
  I saw the world, and yet I was not seen:
My thread is cut, and yet it is not spun;
And now I live, and now my life is done.

I sought my death, and found it in my womb;
  I looked for life, and saw it was a shade;
I trod the earth, and knew it was my tomb;
  And now I die, and now I was but made;
My glass is full, and now my glass is run;
And now I live, and now my life is done.

A BALLADE TO END WITH

Here is poor Villon's final word;
The ink upon his will is dried.
Come see him properly interred
When by the bell you're notified,
And come in scarlet, since he died
Love's martyr, through his gentle heart:
This on one ball he testified
As he made ready to depart.

Nor do I think his claim absurd;
Love hounded him both far and wide,
By such contempt and malice spurred
That, clear to Roussillon, one spied
No thorn in all the countryside
But wore his tattered shirt in part.
So said he (and he never lied)
As he made ready to depart.

And thus and therefore it occurred
That one rag only clothed his hide
When he lay dead; what's more, we heard
How on his bed of death he cried
A pox on Love, who still applied,

Sharper than buckle-tongue, his dart
(A fact which left us saucer-eyed),
As he made ready to depart.

Prince, like a falcon in your pride,
Hear how his pilgrimage did start:
He swigged some dark-red wine, and sighed,
As he made ready to depart.

THE MEDITATION

It must be done (my Soul) but 'tis a strange,
   A dismal and Mysterious Change,
When thou shalt leave this Tenement of Clay,
And to an unknown somewhere wing away;
When Time shall be Eternity, and thou
Shalt be thou know'st not what, and live thou
     know'st not how.

Amazing State! no wonder that we dread
   To think of Death, or view the Dead.
Thou'rt all wrapt up in Clouds, as if to thee
Our very Knowledge had Antipathy.
Death could not a more Sad Retinue find,
Sickness and Pain before, and Darkness all behind.

Some Courteous Ghost, tell this great Secrecy,
   What 'tis you are, and we must be.
You warn us of approaching Death, and why
May we not know from you what 'tis to Dye?
But you, having shot the Gulph, delight to see
Succeeding Souls plunge in with like uncertainty.

When Life's close Knot by Writ from Destiny,
   Disease shall cut, or Age unty;
When after some Delays, some dying Strife,
The Soul stands shivering on the Ridge of Life;
With what a dreadful Curiosity
Does she launch out into the Sea of vast Eternity.

So when the Spatious Globe was delug'd o're,
   And lower holds could save no more,
On th'utmost Bough th'astonish'd Sinners stood,
And view'd th'advances of th'encroaching Flood.
O're-topp'd at length by th'Element's encrease,
With horrour they resign'd to the untry'd Abyss.

ADIEU! FAREWELL EARTH'S BLISS!

Adieu! farewell earth's bliss!
This world uncertain is:
Fond are life's lustful joys,
Death proves them all but toys.
None from his darts can fly:
I am sick, I must die –
   Lord, have mercy on us!

Rich men, trust not in wealth,
Gold cannot buy you health;
Physic himself must fade;
All things to end are made;
The plague full swift goes by:
I am sick, I must die –
   Lord, have mercy on us!

Beauty is but a flower
Which wrinkles will devour:
Brightness falls from the air;
Queens have died young and fair
Dust hath closed Helen's eye:
I am sick, I must die –
   Lord, have mercy on us!

Strength stoops unto the grave
Worms feed on Hector brave;
Sword may not light with fate;
Earth still holds ope her gate;
Come! come! the bells do cry:
I am sick, I must die –
   Lord, have mercy on us!

Wit with his wantonness,
Tasteth death's bitterness;
Hell's executioner
Hath no ears for to hear
What vain art can reply.
I am sick, I must die –
   Lord, have mercy on us!

Haste, therefore, each degree
To welcome destiny!
Heaven is our heritage;
Earth but a player's stage.
Mount we unto the sky!
I am sick, I must die –
   Lord, have mercy on us!

THE FLOWERS OF THE FOREST

I've heard them lilting at our yowe-milking –
   Lasses a-lilting before dawn of day;
But now they are moaning on ilka green loaning –
   The Flowers of the Forest are a' wede away.

At buchts, in the morning, nae blythe lads are
      scorning;
   Lasses are lonely and dowie and wae; –
Nae daffin', nae gabbin' – but sighing and sabbing
   Ilk ane lifts her leglin and hies her away.

In hairst, at the shearing, nae youths now are jerring –
   Bandsters are runkled and lyart or grey:
At fair or at preaching, nae wooing, nae fleeching –
   The Flowers of the Forest are a' wede away.

At e'en, in the gloaming, nae swankies are roaming,
   'Bout stacks with the lasses at bogle to play;
But ilk maid sits drearie, lamenting her dearie –
   The Flowers of the Forest are a' wede away.

Dool and wae for the order sent our lads to the Border!
   The English, for ance, by guile wan the day; –
The Flowers of the Forest, that foucht aye the
      foremost –
   The prime of our land – are cauld in the clay.

We'll hear nae mair lilting at the yowe-milking;
   Women and bairns are heartless and wae,
Sighing and moaning on ilka green loaning –
   The Flowers of the Forest are a' wede away.

DURING WIND AND RAIN

They sing their dearest songs –
He, she, all of them – yea,
Treble and tenor and bass,
    And one to play;
With the candles mooning each face ...
    Ah, no; the years O!
How the sick leaves reel down in throngs!

They clear the creeping moss –
Elders and juniors – aye,
Making the pathways neat
    And the garden gay;
And they build a shady seat ...
    Ah, no; the years, the years;
See, the white storm-birds wing across!

They are blithely breakfasting all –
Men and maidens – yea,
Under the summer tree,
    With a glimpse of the bay,
While pet fowl come to the knee ...
    Ah, no; the years O!
And the rotten rose is ript from the wall.

They change to a high new house,
He, she, all of them – aye,
Clocks and carpets and chairs
　　On the lawn all day,
And brightest things that are theirs ...
　　Ah, no; the years, the years;
Down their carved names the rain-drop ploughs.

ELEGY WRITTEN IN A COUNTRY CHURCHYARD

The curfew tolls the knell of parting day,
The lowing herd wind slowly o'er the lea,
The ploughman homeward plods his weary way,
And leaves the world to darkness and to me.

Now fades the glimmering landscape on the sight,
And all the air a solemn stillness holds,
Save where the beetle wheels his droning flight,
And drowsy tinklings lull the distant folds;

Save that from yonder ivy-mantled tow'r
The moping owl does to the moon complain
Of such as, wand'ring near her secret bow'r,
Molest her ancient solitary reign.

Beneath those rugged elms, that yew-tree's shade,
Where heaves the turf in many a mould'ring heap,
Each in his narrow cell for ever laid,
The rude forefathers of the hamlet sleep.

The breezy call of incense-breathing morn,
The swallow twitt'ring from the straw-built shed,
The cock's shrill clarion or the echoing horn,
No more shall rouse them from their lowly bed.

For them no more the blazing hearth shall burn,
Or busy housewife ply her evening care:
No children run to lisp their sire's return,
Or climb his knees the envied kiss to share.

Oft did the harvest to their sickle yield,
Their furrow oft the stubborn glebe has broke;
How jocund did they drive their team afield!
How bowed the woods beneath their sturdy stroke!

Let not Ambition mock their useful toil,
Their homely joys and destiny obscure;
Nor Grandeur hear, with a disdainful smile,
The short and simple annals of the poor.

The boast of heraldry, the pomp of pow'r,
And all that beauty, all that wealth e'er gave,
Awaits alike the inevitable hour.
The paths of glory lead but to the grave.

Nor you, ye Proud, impute to these the fault,
If Mem'ry o'er their tomb no trophies raise,
Where through the long-drawn aisle and fretted vault
The pealing anthem swells the note of praise.

Can storied urn or animated bust
Back to its mansion call the fleeting breath?

Can Honour's voice provoke the silent dust,
Or Flatt'ry soothe the dull cold ear of Death?

Perhaps in this neglected spot is laid
Some heart once pregnant with celestial fire;
Hands that the rod of empire might have swayed,
Or waked to ecstasy the living lyre.

But Knowledge to their eyes her ample page
Rich with the spoils of time did ne'er unroll;
Chill Penury repressed their noble rage,
And froze the genial current of the soul.

Full many a gem of purest ray serene
The dark unfathomed caves of ocean bear:
Full many a flower is born to blush unseen
And waste its sweetness on the desert air.

Some village-Hampden that with dauntless breast
The little tyrant of his fields withstood;
Some mute inglorious Milton here may rest,
Some Cromwell guiltless of his country's blood.

Th' applause of list'ning senates to command,
The threats of pain and ruin to despise,
To scatter plenty o'er a smiling land,
And read their hist'ry in a nation's eyes,

Their lot forbade: nor circumscribed alone
Their growing virtues, but their crimes confined;
Forbade to wade through slaughter to a throne,
And shut the gates of mercy on mankind,

The struggling pangs of conscious truth to hide,
To quench the blushes of ingenuous shame,
Or heap the shrine of Luxury and Pride
With incense kindled at the Muse's flame.

Far from the madding crowd's ignoble strife
Their sober wishes never learned to stray;
Along the cool sequestered vale of life
They kept the noiseless tenor of their way.

Yet ev'n these bones from insult to protect
Some frail memorial still erected nigh,
With uncouth rhymes and shapeless sculpture decked,
Implores the passing tribute of a sigh.

Their name, their years, spelt by th' unlettered muse,
The place of fame and elegy supply:
And many a holy text around she strews,
That teach the rustic moralist to die.

For who to dumb Forgetfulness a prey,
This pleasing anxious being e'er resigned,

Left the warm precincts of the cheerful day,
Nor cast one longing ling'ring look behind?

On some fond breast the parting soul relies,
Some pious drops the closing eye requires;
Ev'n from the tomb the voice of Nature cries,
Ev'n in our ashes live their wonted fires.

For thee who, mindful of th' unhonoured dead,
Dost in these lines their artless tale relate;
If chance, by lonely Contemplation led,
Some kindred spirit shall inquire thy fate,

Haply some hoary-headed swain may say,
'Oft have we seen him at the peep of dawn
Brushing with hasty steps the dews away
To meet the sun upon the upland lawn.

'There at the foot of yonder nodding beech
That wreathes its old fantastic roots so high,
His listless length at noontide would he stretch,
And pore upon the brook that babbles by.

'Hard by yon wood, now smiling as in scorn,
Muttering his wayward fancies he would rove,
Now drooping, woeful wan, like one forlorn,
Or crazed with care, or crossed in hopeless love.

'One morn I missed him on the customed hill,
Along the heath and near his fav'rite tree;
Another came; nor yet beside the rill,
Nor up the lawn, nor at the wood was he;

'The next with dirges due in sad array
Slow through the church-way path we saw him borne.
Approach and read (for thou canst read) the lay,
Graved on the stone beneath yon aged thorn.'

THE EPITAPH

Here rests his head upon the lap of earth
A youth to fortune and to fame unknown.
Fair Science frowned not on his humble birth,
And Melancholy marked him for her own.

Large was his bounty and his soul sincere,
Heaven did a recompense as largely send:
He gave to Mis'ry all he had, a tear,
He gained from heav'n ('twas all he wished) a friend.

No farther seek his merits to disclose,
Or draw his frailties from their dread abode
(There they alike in trembling hope repose),
The bosom of his Father and his God.

AN ARUNDEL TOMB

Side by side, their faces blurred,
The earl and countess lie in stone,
Their proper habits vaguely shown
As jointed armour, stiffened pleat,
And that faint hint of the absurd –
The little dogs under their feet.

Such plainness of the pre-baroque
Hardly involves the eye, until
It meets his left-hand gauntlet, still
Clasped empty in the other; and
One sees, with a sharp tender shock,
His hand withdrawn, holding her hand.

They would not think to lie so long.
Such faithfulness in effigy
Was just a detail friends would see:
A sculptor's sweet commissioned grace
Thrown off in helping to prolong
The Latin names around the base.

They would not guess how early in
Their supine stationary voyage
The air would change to soundless damage,
Turn the old tenantry away;

How soon succeeding eyes begin
To look, not read. Rigidly they

Persisted, linked, through lengths and breadths
Of time. Snow fell, undated. Light
Each summer thronged the glass. A bright
Litter of birdcalls strewed the same
Bone-riddled ground. And up the paths
The endless altered people came,

Washing at their identity.
Now, helpless in the hollow of
An unarmorial age, a trough
Of smoke in slow suspended skeins
Above their scrap of history,
Only an attitude remains:

Time has transfigured them into
Untruth. The stone fidelity
They hardly meant has come to be
Their final blazon, and to prove
Our almost-instinct almost true:
What will survive of us is love.

MY DEAREST DUST

Epitaph on monument erected in 1641 by
Lady Catherine Dyer to her husband Sir William
Dyer in Colmworth Church, Bedfordshire

My dearest dust, could not thy hasty day
Afford thy drowzy patience leave to stay
One hower longer: so that we might either
Sate up, or gone to bedd together?
But since thy finisht labor hath possest
Thy weary limbs with early rest,
Enjoy it sweetly: and thy widdowe bride
Shall soone repose her by thy slumbering side.
Whose business, now, is only to prepare
My nightly dress, and call to prayre:
Mine eyes wax heavy and ye day growes old.
The dew falls thick, my beloved growes cold.
Draw, draw ye closed curtaynes: and make room:
My dear, my dearest dust; I come, I come.

MARIA WENTWORTH

Thomae *Comitis* Cleveland,
filia praemortua prima
Virgineam animam exhalavit

An. Dom. 1632. Æt. suae 18

And here the precious dust is layd;
Whose purely temper'd Clay was made
So fine, that it the guest betray'd.

Else the soule grew so fast within,
It broke the outward shell of sinne,
And so was hatch'd a Cherubin.

In height, it soar'd to God above;
In depth, it did to knowledge move,
And spread in breadth to generall love.

Before, a pious duty shind
To Parents, courtesie behind,
On either side an equall mind,

Good to the Poore, to kindred deare,
To servants kind, to friendship cleare,
To nothing but her selfe, severe.

So though a Virgin, yet a Bride
To every Grace, she justifi'd
A chaste Poligamie, and dy'd.

Learne from hence (Reader) what small trust
We owe this world, where vertue must
Fraile as our flesh, crumble to dust.

From OVID, TRISTIA III, 3:
To His Wife at Rome, When He was Sick

But thou – for after death I shall be free, –
Fetch home these bones, and what is left of me,
A few flowers give them, with some balm, and lay
Them in some suburb-grave, hard by the way:
And, to inform posterity who's there,
This sad inscription let my marble wear,
'Here lies the soft-soul'd lecturer of love,
Whose envy'd wit did his own ruin prove.
But thou – whoe'er thou beest – that passing by
Lendst to this sudden stone a hasty eye,
If e'er thou knew'st of love the sweet disease,
Grudge not to say, may Ovid rest in peace!'
This for my tomb: but for my books they'll see
More strong and lasting monuments of me,
Which I believe – though fatal – will afford
An endless name unto their ruin'd lord.
And now thus gone, it rests for love of me
Thou shew'st some sorrow to my memory;
Thy funeral offerings to my ashes bear,
With wreaths of cypress bath'd in many a tear.
Though nothing there but dust of me remain,
Yet shall that dust perceive thy pious pain.

But I have done, and my tir'd sickly head,
Though I would fain write more, desires the bed;
Take then this word – perhaps my last to tell –
Which though I want, I wish it thee, farewell!

METHOUGHT I SAW MY LATE ESPOUSÈD SAINT

Methought I saw my late espousèd saint
    Brought to me like Alcestis from the grave,
    Whom Jove's great son to her glad husband gave,
    Rescued from Death by force, though pale and faint.
Mine, as whom washed from spot of child-bed taint
    Purification in the old Law did save,
    And such as yet once more I trust to have
    Full sight of her in heaven without restraint,
Came vested all in white, pure as her mind.
    Her face was veiled; yet to my fancied sight
    Love, sweetness, goodness, in her person shined
So clear as in no face with more delight.
    But O as to embrace me she inclined,
    I waked, she fled, and day brought back my night.

ON PARTING WITH MY WIFE, JANINA

Women mourners were giving their sister to fire.
And fire, the same as we looked at together,
She and I, in marriage through long years,
Bound by an oath for good or ill, fire
In fireplaces in winter, campfires, fires of burning
    cities,
Elemental, pure, from the beginnings of the Earth,
Was taking away her streaming hair, gray,
Seized her lips and her neck, engulfed her, fire
That in human languages designates love.
I thought nothing of languages. Or of words of prayer.

I loved her, without knowing who she really was.
I inflicted pain on her, chasing my illusion.
I betrayed her with women, though faithful to her only.
We lived through much happiness and unhappiness,
Separations, miraculous rescues. And now, this ash.
And the sea battering the shore when I walk the
    empty boulevard.
And the sea battering the shore. And ordinary sorrow.

How to resist nothingness? What power
Preserves what once was, if memory does not last?
For I remember little. I remember so very little.

Indeed, moments restored would mean the
    Last Judgment
That is adjourned from day to day, by Mercy perhaps.

Fire, liberation from gravity. An apple does not fall,
A mountain moves from its place. Beyond the
    fire-curtain,
A lamb stands in the meadow of indestructible forms.
The souls in Purgatory burn. Heraclitus, crazy,
Sees the flame consuming the foundations of the world.
Do I believe in the Resurrection of the Flesh?
    Not of this ash.
I call, I beseech: elements, dissolve yourselves!
Rise into the other, let it come, kingdom!
Beyond the earthly fire compose yourselves anew!

THE WIDOWER

For a season there must be pain –
For a little, little space
I shall lose the sight of her face,
Take back the old life again
While She is at rest in her place.

For a season this pain must endure,
For a little, little while
I shall sigh more often than smile
Till Time shall work me a cure,
And the pitiful days beguile.

For that season we must be apart,
For a little length of years,
Till my life's last hour nears,
And, above the beat of my heart,
I hear Her voice in my ears.

But I shall not understand –
Being set on some later love,
Shall not know her for whom I strove,
Till she reach me forth her hand,
Saying, 'Who but I have the right?'
And out of a troubled night
Shall draw me safe to the land.

RUDYARD KIPLING   109

OVER THE COFFIN

They stand confronting, the coffin between,
His wife of old, and his wife of late,
And the dead man whose they both had been
Seems listening aloof, as to things past date.
– 'I have called,' says the first. 'Do you marvel or not?'
'In truth,' says the second, 'I do – somewhat.'

'Well, there was a word to be said by me! . . .
I divorced that man because of you –
It seemed I must do it, boundenly;
But now I am older, and tell you true,
For life is little, and dead lies he;
I would I had let alone you two!
And both of us, scorning parochial ways,
Had lived like the wives in the patriarchs' days.'

A REFUSAL TO MOURN THE DEATH,
BY FIRE, OF A CHILD IN LONDON

Never until the mankind making
Bird beast and flower
Fathering and all humbling darkness
Tells with silence the last light breaking
And the still hour
Is come of the sea tumbling in harness

And I must enter again the round
Zion of the water bead
And the synagogue of the ear of corn
Shall I let pray the shadow of a sound
Or sow my salt seed
In the least valley of sackcloth to mourn

The majesty and burning of the child's death.
I shall not murder
The mankind of her going with a grave truth
Nor blaspheme down the stations of the breath
With any further
Elegy of innocence and youth.

Deep with the first dead lies London's daughter,
Robed in the long friends,
The grains beyond age, the dark veins of her mother,

Secret by the unmourning water
Of the riding Thames.
After the first death, there is no other.

THE CHILD DYING

Unfriendly friendly universe,
I pack your stars into my purse,
And bid you, bid you so farewell.
That I can leave you, quite go out,
Go out, go out beyond all doubt,
My father says, is the miracle.

You are so great, and I so small:
I am nothing, you are all:
Being nothing, I can take this way.
Oh I need neither rise nor fall,
For when I do not move at all
I shall be out of all your day.

It's said some memory will remain
In the other place, grass in the rain,
Light on the land, sun on the sea,
A flitting grace, a phantom face,
But the world is out. There is no place
Where it and its ghost can ever be.

Father, father, I dread this air
Blown from the far side of despair,
The cold cold corner. What house, what hold,
What hand is there? I look and see

Nothing-filled eternity,
And the great round world grows weak and old.

Hold my hand, oh hold it fast –
I am changing! – until at last
My hand in yours no more will change,
Though yours change on. You here, I there,
So hand in hand, twin-leafed despair –
I did not know death was so strange.

ON MY FIRST SON

Farewell, thou child of my right hand, and joy!
My sin was too much hope of thee, loved boy;
Seven years thou wert lent to me, and I thee pay,
Exacted by thy fate, on the just day.
Oh, could I lose all father now! For why
Will man lament the state he should envy –
To have so soon 'scaped world's and flesh's rage,
And, if no other misery, yet age?
Rest in soft peace, and, asked, say here doth lie
Ben Jonson his best piece of poetry:
For whose sake, henceforth, all his vows be such
As what he loves may never like too much.

EPITAPH UPON A CHILD
THAT DIED

Here she lies, a pretty bud,
Lately made of flesh and blood:
Who as soon fell fast asleep
As her little eyes did peep.
Give her strewings, but not stir
The earth that lightly covers her.

TO MY DEAR SON, GERVASE BEAUMONT

Can I, who have for others oft compiled
The songs of death, forget my sweetest child,
Which, like a flower crushed, with a blast is dead,
And ere full time hangs down his smiling head,
Expecting with clear hope to live anew,
Among the angels fed with heavenly dew?
We have this sign of joy, that many days,
While on the earth his struggling spirit stays,
The name of Jesus in his mouth contains,
His only food, his sleep, his ease from pains.
O may that sound be rooted in my mind,
Of which in him such strong effect I find.
Dear Lord, receive my son, whose winning love
To me was like a friendship, far above
The course of nature, or his tender age;
Whose looks could all my bitter griefs assuage;
Let his pure soul – ordained seven years to be
In that frail body, which was part of me –
Remain my pledge in heaven, as sent to show
How to this port at every step I go.

FLOOD

His home address was inked inside his cap
and on every piece of paper that he carried
even across the church porch of the snap
that showed him with mi mam just minutes married.

But if ah'm found at 'ome (he meant found dead)
turn t'water off. Through his last years he nursed,
more than a fear of dying, a deep dread
of his last bath running over, or a burst.

Each night towards the end he'd pull the flush
then wash, then in pyjamas, rain or snow,
go outside, kneel down in the yard, and push
the stopcock as far off as it would go.

For though hoping that he'd drop off in his sleep
he was most afraid, I think, of not being 'found'
there in their house, his ark, on firm Leeds ground
but somewhere that kept moving, cold, dark, deep.

DO NOT GO GENTLE INTO THAT GOOD NIGHT

Do not go gentle into that good night,
Old age should burn and rave at close of day;
Rage, rage against the dying of the light.

Though wise men at their end know dark is right,
Because their words had forked no lightning they
Do not go gentle into that good night.

Good men, the last wave by, crying how bright
Their frail deeds might have danced in a green bay,
Rage, rage against the dying of the light.

Wild men who caught and sang the sun in flight,
And learn, too late, they grieved it on its way,
Do not go gentle into that good night.

Grave men, near death, who see with blinding sight
Blind eyes could blaze like meteors and be gay,
Rage, rage against the dying of the light.

And you, my father, there on the sad height,
Curse, bless, me now with your fierce tears, I pray.
Do not go gentle into that good night.
Rage, rage against the dying of the light.

DYLAN THOMAS   119

TO HIS DYING BROTHER, MASTER WILLIAM HERRICK

Life of my life, take not so soone thy flight,
But stay the time till we have bade Good night.
Thou hast both Wind and Tide with thee; Thy way
As soone dispatcht is by the Night, as Day.
Let us not then so rudely henceforth goe
Till we have wept, kist, sigh't, shook hands, or so.
There's paine in parting; and a kind of hell,
When once true-lovers take their last Fare-well.
What? shall we two our endlesse leaves take here
Without a sad looke, or a solemne teare?
He knowes not Love, that hath not this truth proved,
Love is most loth to leave the thing beloved.
Pay we our Vowes, and goe; yet when we part,
Then, even then, I will bequeath my heart
Into thy loving hands: For Ile keep none
To warme my Breast, when thou my Pulse art gone.
No, here Ile last, and walk (a harmless shade)
About this Urne, wherein thy Dust is laid,
To guard it so, as nothing here shall be
Heavy, to hurt those sacred seeds of thee.

WITH HER

Those poor, arthritically swollen knees
Of my mother in an absent country.
I think of them on my seventy-fourth birthday
As I attend early Mass at St. Mary Magdalen
    in Berkeley.
A reading this Sunday from the Book of Wisdom
About how God has not made death
And does not rejoice in the annihilation of the living.
A reading from the Gospel according to Mark
About a little girl to whom He said: 'Talitha, cumi!'
This is for me. To make me rise from the dead
And repeat the hope of those who lived before me,
In a fearful unity with her, with her pain of dying,
In a village near Danzig, in a dark November,
When both the mournful Germans, old men
    and women,
And the evacuees from Lithuania would fall ill
    with typhus.
Be with me, I say to her, my time has been short.
Your words are now mine, deep inside me:
'It all seems now to have been a dream.'

UNCLE ANANIAS

His words were magic and his heart was true,
    And everywhere he wandered he was blessed.
Out of all ancient men my childhood knew
    I choose him and I mark him for the best.
Of all authoritative liars, too,
    I crown him loveliest.

How fondly I remember the delight
    That always glorified him in the spring;
The joyous courage and the benedight
    Profusion of his faith in everything!
He was a good old man, and it was right
    That he should have his fling.

And often, underneath the apple-trees,
    When we surprised him in the summer time,
With what superb magnificence and ease
    He sinned enough to make the day sublime!
And if he liked us there about his knees,
    Truly it was no crime.

All summer long we loved him for the same
    Perennial inspiration of his lies;
And when the russet wealth of autumn came,
    There flew but fairer visions to our eyes –

Multiple, tropical, winged with a feathery flame,
   Like birds of paradise.

So to the sheltered end of many a year
   He charmed the seasons out with pageantry
Wearing upon his forehead, with no fear,
   The laurel of approved iniquity.
And every child who knew him, far or near,
   Did love him faithfully.

ELEGY

Her face like a rain-beaten stone on the day she rolled off
With the dark hearse, and enough flowers for an
     alderman, –
And so she was, in her way, Aunt Tilly.

Sighs, sighs, who says they have sequence?
Between the spirit and the flesh, – what war?
She never knew;
For she asked no quarter and gave none,
Who sat with the dead when the relatives left,
Who fed and tended the infirm, the mad, the epileptic,
And, with a harsh rasp of a laugh at herself,
Faced up to the worst.

I recall how she harried the children away all the late
     summer
From the one beautiful thing in her yard, the
     peachtree;
How she kept the wizened, the fallen, the misshapen
     for herself,
And picked and pickled the best, to be left on rickety
     doorsteps.

And yet she died in agony,
Her tongue, at the last, thick, black as an ox's.

Terror of cops, bill collectors, betrayers of the poor, –
I see you in some celestial supermarket,
Moving serenely among the leeks and cabbages,
Probing the squash,
Bearing down, with two steady eyes,
On the quaking butcher.

BY HER AUNT'S GRAVE

'Sixpence a week', says the girl to her lover,
'Aunt used to bring me, for she could confide
In me alone, she vowed. 'Twas to cover
The cost of her headstone when she died.
And that was a year ago last June;
I've not yet fixed it. But I must soon.'

'And where is the money now, my dear?'
'O, snug in my purse . . . Aunt was *so* slow
In saving it – eighty weeks, or near.'. . .
'Let's spend it,' he hints. 'For she won't know.
There's a dance to-night at the Load of Hay.'
She passively nods. And they go that way.

COOTCHIE

Cootchie, Miss Lula's servant, lies in marl,
black into white she went
     below the surface of the coral-reef.
Her life was spent
     in caring for Miss Lula, who is deaf,
eating her dinner off the kitchen sink
while Lula ate hers off the kitchen table.
The skies were egg-white for the funeral
     and the faces sable.

Tonight the moonlight will alleviate
the melting of the pink wax roses
     planted in tin cans filled with sand
placed in a line to mark Miss Lula's losses;
     but who will shout and make her understand?
Searching the land and sea for someone else,
the lighthouse will discover Cootchie's grave
and dismiss all as trivial; the sea, desperate,
     will proffer wave after wave.

FELIX RANDAL

Felix Randal the farrier, O he is dead then?
    my duty all ended,
Who have watched his mould of man,
    big-boned and hardy-handsome
Pining, pining, till time when reason rambled
    in it and some
Fatal four disorders, fleshed there, all contended?

Sickness broke him. Impatient he cursed at first,
    but mended
Being anointed and all; though a heavenlier heart
    began some
Months earlier, since I had our sweet reprieve
    and ransom
Tendered to him. Ah well, God rest him all road
    ever he offended!

This seeing the sick endears them to us,
    us too it endears.
My tongue had taught thee comfort,
    touch had quenched thy tears,
Thy tears that touched my heart, child, Felix,
    poor Felix Randal;

How far from then forethought of,
   all thy more boisterous years,
When thou at the random grim forge,
   powerful amidst peers,
Didst fettle for the great grey drayhorse his bright
   and battering sandal!

REQUIEM FOR A FRIEND

I have my dead, and I would let them go
and be surprised to see them all so cheerful,
so soon at home in being-dead, so right,
so unlike their repute. You, you alone,
return; brush past me, move about, persist
in knocking something that vibratingly
betrays you. Oh, don't take from me what I
am slowly learning. I'm right; you're mistaken,
if you're disturbed into a home-sick longing
for something here. We transmute it all;
it's not here, we reflect it from ourselves,
from our own being, as soon as we perceive it.

    I thought you'd got much further. It confounds me
that *you* should thus mistake and come, who passed
all other women so in transmutation.
That we were frightened when you died, or, rather,
that your strong death made a dark interruption,
tearing the till-then from the ever-since:
that is our business: to set that in order
will be the work that everything provides us.
But that you too were frightened, even now
are frightened, now, when fright has lost its meaning,
that you are losing some of your eternity,
even a little, to step in here, friend, here,
where nothing yet exists; that in the All,

for the first time distracted and half-hearted,
you did not grasp the infinite ascension
as once you grasped each single thing on earth;
that from the orbit that already held you
the gravitation of some mute unrest
should drag you down to measurable time:
this often wakes me like an entering thief.
If I could say you merely deign to come
from magnanimity, from superabundance,
because you are so sure, so self-possessed,
that you can wander like a child, not frightened
of places where ther're things that happen to one –
but no, you're asking. And that penetrates
right to the bone and rattles like a saw.
Reproach, such as you might bear as a spirit,
bear against me when I withdraw myself
at night into my lungs, into my bowels,
into the last poor chamber of my heart,
such a reproach would not be half so cruel
as this mute asking. What is it you ask?

   Say, shall I travel? Have you left somewhere
a thing behind you, that torments itself
with trying to reach you? Travel to a country
you never saw, although it was as closely
akin to you as one half of your senses?

   I'll voyage on its rivers, set my foot
upon its soil and ask about old customs,

stand talking with the women in their doorways
and pay attention when they call their children.
I will observe how they take on the landscape
outside there in the course of the old labour
of field and meadow; will express a wish
to be presented to the king himself,
and work upon the priests with bribery
to leave me lying before the strongest statue
and then withdraw, shutting the temple doors.
But in conclusion, having learnt so much,
I'll simply watch the animals, that something
of their own way of turning may glide over
into my joints; I'll have a brief existence
within their eyes, that solemnly retain me
and slowly loose me, calmly, without judgement.
I'll make the gardeners repeat by heart
the names of many flowers and so bring back
in pots of lovely proper names a remnant,
a little remnant, of the hundred perfumes.
And I will purchase fruits too, fruits, wherein
that country, sky and all, will re-exist.

For that was what you understood: full fruits.
You used to set them out in bowls before you
and counterpoise their heaviness with colours.
And women too appeared to you as fruits,
and children too, both of them from within
impelled into the forms of their existence.

And finally you saw yourself as fruit,
lifted yourself out of your clothes and carried
that self before the mirror, let it in
up to your gaze; which remained, large, in front,
and did not say: that's me; no, but: this is.
So uninquiring was your gaze at last,
so unpossessive and so truly poor,
it wanted even you no longer: holy.

That's how I would retain you, as you placed
yourself within the mirror, deep within,
and far from all else. Why come differently?
Why thus revoke yourself? Why are you trying
to make me feel that in those amber beads
around your neck there was still something heavy
with such a heaviness as never lurks
in the beyond of tranquil pictures? Why
does something in your bearing bode misfortune?
What makes you read the contours of your body
like lines upon a hand, and me no longer
able to see them but as destiny?

Come to the candle-light. I'm not afraid
to look upon the dead. When they return
they have a right to hospitality
within our gaze, the same as other things.

Come; we'll remain a little while in silence.
Look at this rose, here on my writing-desk:
is not the light around it just as timid

as that round you? It too should not be here.
It ought to have remained or passed away
out in the garden there, unmixed with me –
it stays, unconscious of my consciousness.

Don't be afraid now if I comprehend:
it's rising in me – oh, I must, I must,
even if it kills me, I must comprehend.
Comprehend, that you're here. I comprehend.
Just as a blind man comprehends a thing,
I feel your fate although I cannot name it.
Let both of us lament that someone took you
out of your mirror. If you still can cry?
No, you can't cry. You long ago transformed
the force and thrust of tears to your ripe gazing,
and were in act of changing every kind
of sap within you to a strong existence
that mounts and circles in blind equipoise.
Then, for the last time, chance got hold of you,
and snatched you back out of your farthest progress,
back to a world where saps will have their way.
Did not snatch all, only a piece at first,
but when reality, from day to day,
so swelled around that piece that it grew heavy,
you needed your whole self; then off you went
and broke yourself in fragments from your law,
laboriously, needing yourself. And then

you took yourself away and from your heart's
warm, night-warm, soil you dug the yet green seeds
your death was going to spring from: your own death,
the death appropriate to your own life.
And then you ate those grains of your own death
like any others, ate them one by one,
and had within yourself an after-taste
of unexpected sweetness, had sweet lips,
you: in your senses sweet within already.

Let us lament. Do you know how unwilling
and hesitatingly your blood returned,
recalled from an incomparable orbit?
With what confusion it took up again
the tiny circulation of the body?
With what mistrust it entered the placenta,
suddenly tired from the long homeward journey?
You drove it on again, you pushed it forward,
you dragged it to the hearth, as people drag
a herd of animals to sacrifice;
and spite of all desired it to be happy.
And finally you forced it: it was happy,
and ran up and surrendered. You supposed,
being so accustomed to the other measures,
that this was only for a little while;
but now you were in time, and time is long.
And time goes by, and time goes on, and time
is like relapsing after some long illness.

How very short your life, when you compare it
with hours you used to sit in silence, bending
the boundless forces of your boundless future
out of their course to the new germination,
that became fate once more. O painful labour.
Labour beyond all strength. And you performed it
day after day, you dragged yourself along to it
and pulled the lovely wool out of the loom
and wove your threads into another pattern.
And still had spirit for a festival.

For when you'd done you looked for some reward,
like children, when they've drunk a nasty drink
of bitter-sweet tea that may make one better.
You gave your own reward, being still so distant,
even then, from all the rest; and no one there
who could have hit on a reward to please you.
You yourself knew it. You sat up in child-bed,
a mirror there before you, that returned
all that you gave. Now everything was you,
and right in front; within was mere deceit,
the sweet deceit of Everywoman, gladly
putting her jewels on and doing her hair.

And so you died like women long ago,
died in the old warm house, old-fashionedly,
the death of those in child-bed, who are trying
to close themselves again but cannot do it,
because that darkness which they also bore

returns and grows importunate and enters.

Ought they not, though, to have gone and hunted up
some mourners for you? Women who will weep
for money, and, if paid sufficiently,
will howl through a whole night when all is still.
Observances! We haven't got enough
observances. All vanishes in talk.
That's why you have to come back, and with me
retrieve omitted mourning. Can you hear me?
I'd like to fling my voice out like a cloth
over the broken fragments of your death
and tug at it till it was all in tatters,
and everything I said was forced to go
clad in the rags of that torn voice and freeze –
if mourning were enough. But I accuse:
not him who thus withdrew you from yourself
(I can't distinguish him, he's like them all),
but in him I accuse all: accuse man.

If somewhere deep within me rises up
a having-once-been-child I don't yet know,
perhaps the purest childness of my childhood:
I will not know it. Without looking at it
or asking, I will make an angel of it,
and hurl that angel to the foremost rank
of crying angels that remembrance God.

For now too long this suffering has lasted,

and none can stand it; it's too hard for us,
this tortuous suffering caused by spurious love,
which, building on prescription like a habit,
calls itself just and battens on injustice.
Where is the man who justly may possess?
Who can possess what cannot hold itself
but only now and then blissfully catches
and flings itself on like a child a ball?
As little as the admiral can retain
the Nikê poised upon his vessel's prow
when the mysterious lightness of her godhead
has caught her up into the limpid sea-wind,
can one of us call back to him the woman
who, seeing us no longer, takes her way
along some narrow strip of her existence,
as though a miracle, without mischance –
unless his calling and delight were guilt.

   For this is guilt, if anything be guilt,
not to enlarge the freedom of a love
with all the freedom in one's own possession.
All we can offer where we love is this:
to loose each other; for to hold each other
comes easy to us and requires no learning.

Are you still there? Still hiding in some corner? –
You knew so much of all that I've been saying,
and could so much too, for you passed through life

open to all things, like a breaking day.
Women suffer: loving means being lonely,
and artists feel at times within their work
the need, where most they love, for transmutation.
You began both; and both exist in *that*
which fame, detaching it from you, disfigures.
Oh, you were far beyond all fame. Were in-
conspicuous; had gently taken in
your beauty as a gala flag's intaken
on the grey morning of a working-day,
and wanted nothing but a lengthy work –
which is not done; in spite of all, not done.

   If you're still there, if somewhere in this darkness
there's still a spot where your perceptive spirit's
vibrating on the shallow waves of sound
a lonely voice within a lonely night
starts in the air-stream of a lofty room:
hear me and help me. Look, without knowing when,
we keep on slipping backwards from our progress
into some unintended thing, and there
we get ourselves involved as in a dream,
and there at last we die without awakening.
No one's got further. Anyone who's lifted
the level of his blood to some long work
may find he's holding it aloft no longer
and that it's worthlessly obeying its weight.
For somewhere there's an old hostility

between our human life and greatest work.
May I see into it and it say: help me!

Do not return. If you can bear it, stay
dead with the dead. The dead are occupied.
But help me, as you may without distraction,
as the most distant sometimes helps: in me.

TO A FRIEND: IN MEMORIAM

It's for you whose name's better omitted – since for
      them it's no arduous task
to produce you from under the slab – from one more
      inconnu: me, well, partly
for the same earthly reasons, since they'll scrub you as
      well off the cask,
and because I'm up here and, frankly, apart from this
      paltry
talk of slabs, am too distant for you to distinguish a voice,
an Aesopian chant, in that homeland of bottle-struck
      livers,
where you fingered your course to the pole in the moist
      universe
of mean, blabbering squinchers and whispering, innocent
      beavers;
it's for you, name omitted, the offspring of a widowed
      conductress, begot
by the Holy Ghost or by brick courtyard's soot circling
      all over,
an abductor of books, the sharp pen of the most
      smashing ode
on the fall of the bard at the feet of the laced Goncharova,
a word-plyer, a liar, a gulper of bright, measly tears,
an adorer of Ingres, of clangoring streetcars, of asphodels'
      slumbers,

a white-fanged little snake in the tarpaulin-boot
    colonnade of gendarmes in full gear,
a monogamous heart and a torso of countless
    bedchambers –
may you lie, as though wrapped in an Orenburg shawl,
    in our dry, brownish mud,
you, a tramper through hell and high water and the
    meaningless sentence,
who took life like a bumblebee touching a sun-heated
    bud
but instead froze to death in the Third Rome's cold-
    piss-reeking entrance.
Maybe Nothing has no better gateway indeed than this
    smelly shortcut.
Man of sidewalks, you'd say, 'This will do,' adding, 'for
    the duration,'
as you drifted along the dark river in your ancient gray,
    drab overcoat
whose few buttons alone were what kept you from
    disintegration.
Gloomy Charon in vain seeks the coin in your tightly
    shut shell,
someone's pipe blows in vain its small tune far above
    heavy, cumulous curtains.
With a bow, I bid you this anonymous, muted farewell
from the shores – who knows which? Though for you
    now it has no importance.

IN MEMORY OF EVA GORE-BOOTH
AND CON MARKIEWICZ

The light of evening, Lissadell,
Great windows open to the south,
Two girls in silk kimonos, both
Beautiful, one a gazelle.
But a raving autumn shears
Blossom from the summer's wreath;
The older is condemned to death,
Pardoned, drags out lonely years
Conspiring among the ignorant.
I know not what the younger dreams –
Some vague Utopia – and she seems,
When withered old and skeleton-gaunt,
An image of such politics.
Many a time I think to seek
One or the other out and speak
Of that old Georgian mansion, mix
Pictures of the mind, recall
That table and the talk of youth,
Two girls in silk kimonos, both
Beautiful, one a gazelle.

Dear shadows, now you know it all,
All the folly of a fight
With a common wrong or right.

The innocent and the beautiful
Have no enemy but time;
Arise and bid me strike a match
And strike another till time catch;
Should the conflagration climb,
Run till all the sages know.
We the great gazebo built,
They convicted us of guilt;
Bid me strike a match and blow.

WHEN LILACS LAST IN THE DOORYARD BLOOM'D

I

When lilacs last in the dooryard bloom'd,
And the great star early droop'd in the western sky in
the night,
I mourn'd, and yet shall mourn with ever-returning
spring.

Ever-returning spring, trinity sure to me you bring,
Lilac blooming perennial and drooping star in the
west,
And thought of him I love.

II

O powerful western fallen star!
O shades of night – O moody, tearful night!
O great star disappear'd – O the black murk that hides
the star!
O cruel hands that hold me powerless – O helpless soul
of me!
O harsh surrounding cloud that will not free my soul.

III

In the dooryard fronting an old farm-house near the
      white-wash'd palings,
Stands the lilac-bush tall-growing with heart-shaped
      leaves of rich green,
With many a pointed blossom rising delicate, with the
      perfume strong I love,
With every leaf a miracle – and from this bush in the
      dooryard,
With delicate-color'd blossoms and heart-shaped
      leaves of rich green,
A sprig with its flower I break.

IV

In the swamp in secluded recesses,
A shy and hidden bird is warbling a song.

Solitary the thrush,
The hermit withdrawn to himself; avoiding the
      settlements,
Sings by himself a song.

Song of the bleeding throat,
Death's outlet song of life, (for well dear brother I
      know,
If thou wast not granted to sing thou would'st surely
      die.)

V

Over the breast of the spring, the land, amid cities,
Amid lanes and through old woods, where lately the
      violets peep'd from the ground, spotting the gray
      debris,
Amid the grass in the fields each side of the lanes,
      passing the endless grass,
Passing the yellow-spear'd wheat, every grain from its
      shroud in the dark-brown fields uprisen,
Passing the apple-tree blows of white and pink in the
      orchards,
Carrying a corpse to where it shall rest in the
      grave,
Night and day journeys a coffin.

VI

Coffin that passes through lanes and streets,
Through day and night with the great cloud darkening
      the land,
With the pomp of the inloop'd flags with the cities
      draped in black,
With the show of the States themselves as of
      crape-veil'd women standing,
With processions long and winding and the flambeaus
      of the night,
With the countless torches lit, with the silent sea of
      faces and the unbared heads,

With the waiting depot, the arriving coffin, and the
    sombre faces,
With dirges through the night, with the thousand
    voices rising strong and solemn,
With all the mournful voices of the dirges pour'd
    around the coffin,
The dim-lit churches and the shuddering organs –
    where amid these you journey,
With the tolling tolling bells' perpetual clang,
Here, coffin that slowly passes,
I give you my sprig of lilac.

VII

(Nor for you, for one alone,
Blossoms and branches green to coffins all I bring,
For fresh as the morning, thus would I chant a song for
    you O sane and sacred death.

All over bouquets of roses,
O death, I cover you over with roses and early lilies,
But mostly and now the lilac that blooms the first,
Copious I break, I break the sprigs from the bushes,
With loaded arms I come, pouring for you,
For you and the coffins all of you O death.)

VIII

O western orb sailing the heaven,
Now I know what you must have meant as a month
    since I walk'd,
As I walk'd in silence the transparent shadowy night,
As I saw you had something to tell as you bent to me
    night after night,
As you droop'd from the sky low down as if to my side,
    (while the other stars all look'd on,)
As we wander'd together the solemn night, (for
    something I know not what kept me from sleep,)
As the night advanced, and I saw on the rim of the west
    how full you were of woe,
As I stood on the rising ground in the breeze in the
    cool transparent night,
As I watch'd where you pass'd and was lost in the
    netherward black of the night,
As my soul in its trouble dissatisfied sank, as where
    you sad orb,
Concluded, dropt in the night, and was gone.

IX

Sing on there in the swamp,
O singer bashful and tender, I hear your notes, I hear
    your call,
I hear, I come presently, I understand you,

But a moment I linger, for the lustrous star has
    detain'd me,
The star my departing comrade holds and detains me.

X

O how shall I warble myself for the dead one there
    I loved?
And how shall I deck my song for the large sweet soul
    that has gone?
And what shall my perfume be for the grave of him
    I love?

Sea-winds blown from east and west,
Blown from the Eastern sea and blown from the
    Western sea, till there on the prairies meeting,
These and with these and the breath of my chant,
I'll perfume the grave of him I love.

XI

O what shall I hang on the chamber walls?
And what shall the pictures be that I hang on the walls,
To adorn the burial-house of him I love?

Pictures of growing spring and farms and homes,
With the Fourth-month eve at sundown, and the gray
    smoke lucid and bright,

With floods of the yellow gold of the gorgeous,
    indolent, sinking sun, burning, expanding the air,
With the fresh sweet herbage under foot, and the pale
    green leaves of the trees prolific,
In the distance the flowing glaze, the breast of the
    river, with a wind-dapple here and there,
With ranging hills on the banks, with many a line
    against the sky, and shadows,
And the city at hand with dwellings so dense, and
    stacks of chimneys,
And all the scenes of life and the workshops, and the
    workmen homeward returning.

XII

Lo, body and soul – this land,
My own Manhattan with spires, and the sparkling and
    hurrying tides, and the ships,
The varied and ample land, the South and the North in
    the light, Ohio's shores and flashing Missouri,
And ever the far-spreading prairies cover'd with grass
    and corn.

Lo, the most excellent sun so calm and haughty,
The violet and purple morn with just-felt breezes,
The gentle soft-born measureless light,
The miracle spreading bathing all, the fulfill'd noon,

The coming eve delicious, the welcome night and the
    stars,
Over my cities shining all, enveloping man and land.

XIII

Sing on, sing on you gray-brown bird,
Sing from the swamps, the recesses, pour your chant
    from the bushes,
Limitless out of the dusk, out of the cedars and pines.

Sing on dearest brother, warble your reedy song,
Loud human song, with voice of uttermost woe.

O liquid and free and tender!
O wild and loose to my soul – O wondrous singer!
You only I hear – yet the star holds me, (but will soon
    depart,)
Yet the lilac with mastering odor holds me.

XIV

Now while I sat in the day and look'd forth,
In the close of the day with its light and the fields of
    spring, and the farmers preparing their crops,
In the large unconscious scenery of my land with its
    lakes and forests,
In the heavenly aerial beauty, (after the perturb'd
    winds and the storms,)

Under the arching heavens of the afternoon swift
      passing, and the voices of children and women,
The many-moving sea-tides, and I saw the ships how
      they sail'd,
And the summer approaching with richness, and the
      fields all busy with labor,
And the infinite separate houses, how they all went on,
      each with its meals and minutia of daily usages,
And the streets how their throbbings throbb'd, and the
      cities pent – lo, then and there,
Falling upon them all and among them all, enveloping
      me with the rest,
Appear'd the cloud, appear'd the long black trail,
And I knew death, its thought, and the sacred
      knowledge of death.

Then with the knowledge of death as walking one side
      of me,
And the thought of death close-walking the other side
      of me,
And I in the middle as with companions, and as
      holding the hands of companions,
I fled forth to the hiding receiving night that talks not,
Down to the shores of the water, the path by the
      swamp in the dimness,
To the solemn shadowy cedars and ghostly pines so
      still.

And the singer so shy to the rest receiv'd me,
The gray-brown bird I know receiv'd us comrades
    three,
And he sang the carol of death, and a verse for him
    I love.

From deep secluded recesses,
From the fragrant cedars and the ghostly pines so still,
Came the carol of the bird.

And the charm of the carol rapt me,
As I held as if by their hands my comrades in the night,
And the voice of my spirit tallied the song of the bird.

Come lovely and soothing death,
Undulate round the world, serenely arriving, arriving,
In the day, in the night, to all, to each,
Sooner or later delicate death.

Prais'd be the fathomless universe,
For life and joy, and for objects and knowledge curious,
And for love, sweet love – but praise! praise! praise!
For the sure-enwinding arms of cool-enfolding death.

Dark mother always gliding near with soft feet,
Have none chanted for thee a chant of fullest welcome?
Then I chant it for thee, I glorify thee above all,
I bring thee a song that when thou must indeed come, come
      unfalteringly.

Approach strong deliveress,
When it is so, when thou hast taken them I joyously sing the
      dead,
Lost in the loving floating ocean of thee,
Laved in the flood of thy bliss O death.

From me to thee glad serenades,
Dances for thee I propose saluting thee, adornments and
      feastings for thee,
And the sights of the open landscape and the high-spread sky
      are fitting,
And life and the fields, and the huge and thoughtful night.

The night in silence under many a star,
The ocean shore and the husky whispering wave whose voice
      I know,
And the soul turning to thee O vast and well-veil'd death,
And the body gratefully nestling close to thee.

Over the tree-tops I float thee a song,
Over the rising and sinking waves, over the myriad fields
and the prairies wide,
Over the dense-pack'd cities all and the teeming wharves
and ways,
I float this carol with joy, with joy to thee O death.

XV

To the tally of my soul,
Loud and strong kept up the gray-brown bird,
With pure deliberate notes spreading filling the night.

Loud in the pines and cedars dim,
Clear in the freshness moist and the swamp-perfume,
And I with my comrades there in the night.

While my sight that was bound in my eyes unclosed,
As to long panoramas of visions.

And I saw askant the armies,
I saw as in noiseless dreams hundreds of battle-flags,
Borne through the smoke of the battles and pierc'd
with missiles I saw them,
And carried hither and yon through the smoke, and
torn and bloody,
And at last but a few shreds left on the staffs, (and all in
silence,)
And the staffs all splinter'd and broken.

I saw battle-corpses, myriads of them,
And the white skeletons of young men, I saw them,
I saw the debris and debris of all the slain soldiers of
    the war,
But I saw they were not as was thought,
They themselves were fully at rest, they suffer'd not,
The living remain'd and suffer'd, the mother suffer'd,
And the wife and the child and the musing comrade
    suffer'd,
And the armies that remain'd suffer'd.

XVI

Passing the visions, passing the night,
Passing, unloosing the hold of my comrades' hands,
Passing the song of the hermit bird and the tallying
    song of my soul,
Victorious song, death's outlet song, yet varying ever-
    altering song,
As low and wailing, yet clear the notes, rising and
    falling, flooding the night,
Sadly sinking and fainting, as warning and warning,
    and yet again bursting with joy,
Covering the earth and filling the spread of the heaven,
As that powerful psalm in the night I heard from
    recesses,
Passing, I leave thee lilac with heart-shaped leaves,
I leave thee there in the door-yard, blooming,
    returning with spring.

157

I cease from my song for thee,
From my gaze on thee in the west, fronting the west,
    communing with thee,
O comrade lustrous with silver face in the night.

Yet each to keep and all, retrievements out of the night,
The song, the wondrous chant of the gray-brown bird,
And the tallying chant, the echo arous'd in my soul,
With the lustrous and drooping star with the
    countenance full of woe,
With the holders holding my hand nearing the call of
    the bird,
Comrades mine and I in the midst, and their memory
    ever to keep, for the dead I loved so well,
For the sweetest, wisest soul of all my days and lands –
    and this for his dear sake,
Lilac and star and bird twined with the chant of my
    soul,
There in the fragrant pines and the cedars dusk and
    dim.

THE POET'S DEATH

He lay. His high-propped face could only peer
in pale refusal at the silent cover,
now that the world and all this knowledge of her,
torn from the senses of her lover,
had fallen back to the unfeeling year.

Those who had seen him living saw no trace
of his deep unity with all that passes;
for these, these valleys here, these meadow-grasses,
these streams of running water, *were* his face.

Oh yes, his face was this remotest distance,
that seeks him still and woos him in despair;
and his mere mask, timidly dying there,
tender and open, has no more consistence
than broken fruit corrupting in the air.

RAINER MARIA RILKE
TRANS. J. B. LEISHMAN

THE CHOIRMASTER'S BURIAL

He often would ask us
That, when he died,
After playing so many
To their last rest,
If out of us any
Should here abide,
And it would not task us,
We would with our lutes
Play over him
By his grave-brim
The psalm he liked best –
The one whose sense suits
'Mount Ephraim' –
And perhaps we should seem
To him, in Death's dream,
Like the seraphim.

As soon as I knew
That his spirit was gone
I thought this his due,
And spoke thereupon.
'I think,' said the vicar,
'A read service quicker
Than viols out-of-doors
In these frosts and hoars.

That old-fashioned way
Requires a fine day,
And it seems to me
It had better not be.'

Hence, that afternoon,
Though never knew he
That his wish could not be,
To get through it faster
They buried the master
Without any tune.

But 'twas said that, when
At the dead of next night
The vicar looked out,
There struck on his ken
Thronged roundabout,
Where the frost was graying
The headstoned grass,
A band all in white
Like the saints in church-glass,
Singing and playing
The ancient stave
By the choirmaster's grave.

Such the tenor man told
When he had grown old.

THOMAS HARDY   161

AT MELVILLE'S TOMB

Often beneath the wave, wide from this ledge
The dice of drowned men's bones he saw bequeath
An embassy. Their numbers as he watched,
Beat on the dusty shore and were obscured.

And wrecks passed without sound of bells,
The calyx of death's bounty giving back
A scattered chapter, livid hieroglyph,
The portent wound in corridors of shells.

Then in the circuit calm of one vast coil,
Its lashings charmed and malice reconciled,
Frosted eyes there were that lifted altars;
And silent answers crept across the stars.

Compass, quadrant and sextant contrive
No farther tides ... High in the azure steeps
Monody shall not wake the mariner.
This fabulous shadow only the sea keeps.

AT THE GRAVE OF HENRY JAMES

The snow, less intransigent than their marble,
Has left the defence of whiteness to these tombs,
    And all the pools at my feet
Accommodate blue now, echo such clouds as occur
To the sky, and whatever bird or mourner the passing
    Moment remarks they repeat.

While rocks, named after singular spaces
Within which images wandered once that caused
    All to tremble and offend,
Stand here in an innocent stillness, each marking
      the spot
Where one more series of errors lost its uniqueness
    And novelty came to an end.

To whose real advantage were such transactions,
When worlds of reflection were exchanged for trees?
    What living occasion can
Be just to the absent? Noon but reflects on itself,
And the small taciturn stone, that is the only witness
    To a great and talkative man,

Has no more judgement than my ignorant shadow
Of odious comparisons or distant clocks
    Which challenge and interfere

With the heart's instantaneous reading of time,
  time that is
A warm enigma no longer to you for whom I
  Surrender my private cheer,

As I stand awake on our solar fabric,
That primary machine, the earth, which gendarmes,
  banks
  And aspirin pre-suppose,
On which the clumsy and sad may all sit down, and
  any who will
Say their a-ha to the beautiful, the common locus
  Of the Master and the rose.

Shall I not especially bless you as, vexed with
My little inferior questions, I stand
  Above the bed where you rest,
Who opened such passionate arms to your *Bon* when
  It ran
Towards you with its overwhelming reasons pleading
  All beautifully in Its breast?

With what an innocence your hand submitted
To those formal rules that help a child to play,
  While your heart, fastidious as
A delicate nun, remained true to the rare noblesse
Of your lucid gift and, for its love, ignored the
  Resentful muttering Mass,

Whose ruminant hatred of all that cannot
Be simplified or stolen is yet at large:
   No death can assuage its lust
To vilify the landscape of Distinction and see
The heart of the Personal brought to a systolic
     standstill,
   The Tall to diminished dust.

Preserve me, Master, from its vague incitement;
Yours be the disciplinary image that holds
   Me back from agreeable wrong
And the clutch of eddying Muddle, lest Proportion
     shed
The alpine chill of her shrugging editorial shoulder
   On my loose impromptu song.

All will be judged. Master of nuance and scruple,
Pray for me and for all writers, living or dead:
   Because there are many whose works
Are in better taste than their lives, because there is
     no end
To the vanity of our calling, make intercession
   For the treason of all clerks.

LAMENT FOR LU YIN

Poets are usually pure, rugged,
Die from hunger, cling to desolate mountains.
Since this white cloud had no master,
When it flew off, its mind was free from care.
After long sickness, a corpse on a bed,
The servant boy too weak to manage the funeral.
Your old books, all gnawed by famished rats,
Lie strewn and scattered in your single room.
As you go off to the land of new ghosts,
I look on your features white as old jade.
I am ashamed that, when you enter the earth,
No one calls after you, to hold you back.
All the springs lament for you in vain,
As the day lengthens, murmuring waters mourn.

TRANS. STEPHEN OWEN

LYCIDAS

In this monody the author bewails a learned friend,
unfortunately drowned in his passage from Chester on the
Irish Seas, 1637; and, by occasion, foretells the ruin of our
corrupted clergy, then in their height.

Yet once more, O ye laurels, and once more
Ye myrtles brown, with ivy never sere,
I come to pluck your berries harsh and crude,
And with forced fingers rude
Shatter your leaves before the mellowing year.
Bitter constraint and sad occasion dear
Compels me to disturb your season due;
For Lycidas is dead, dead ere his prime,
Young Lycidas, and hath not left his peer.
Who would not sing for Lycidas? He knew
Himself to sing, and build the lofty rhyme.
He must not float upon his watery bier
Unwept, and welter to the parching wind,
Without the meed of some melodious tear.
    Begin, then, sisters of the sacred well
That from beneath the seat of Jove doth spring;
Begin, and somewhat loudly sweep the string.
Hence with denial vain and coy excuse;
So may some gentle muse
With lucky words favour my destined urn,
And as he passes turn,

And bid fair peace be to my sable shroud.

For we were nursed upon the self-same hill,
Fed the same flock, by fountain, shade, and rill;
Together both, ere the high lawns appeared
Under the opening eyelids of the morn,
We drove a-field, and both together heard
What time the grey-fly winds her sultry horn,
Battening our flocks with the fresh dews of night,
Oft till the star that rose, at evening, bright,
Toward heaven's descent had sloped his westering
        wheel.
Meanwhile the rural ditties were not mute;
Tempered to the oaten flute,
Rough satyrs danced, and fauns with cloven heel
From the glad sound would not be absent long;
And old Damaetus loved to hear our song.

But O the heavy change, now thou art gone,
Now thou art gone and never must return!
Thee, shepherd, thee the woods and desert caves,
With wild thyme and the gadding vine o'ergrown,
And all their echoes, mourn.
The willows, and the hazel copses green,
Shall now no more be seen
Fanning their joyous leaves to thy soft lays.
As killing as the canker to the rose,
Or taint-worm to the weanling herds that graze,
Or frost to flowers, that their gay wardrobe wear,

When first the white-thorn blows;
Such, Lycidas, thy loss to shepherd's ear.

Where were ye, nymphs, when the remorseless deep
Closed o'er the head of your loved Lycidas?
For neither were ye playing on the steep
Where your old bards, the famous Druids, lie,
Nor on the shaggy top of Mona high,
Nor yet where Deva spreads her wizard stream.
Ay me! I fondly dream
'Had ye been there,' ... for what could that have done?
What could the muse herself that Orpheus bore,
The muse herself, for her enchanting son,
Whom universal nature did lament,
When, by the rout that made the hideous roar,
His gory visage down the stream was sent,
Down the swift Hebrus to the Lesbian shore?

Alas! What boots it with uncessant care
To tend the homely slighted shepherd's trade,
And strictly meditate the thankless muse?
Were it not better done, as others use,
To sport with Amaryllis in the shade,
Or with the tangles of Neaera's hair?
Fame is the spur that the clear spirit doth raise
(That last infirmity of noble mind)
To scorn delights and live laborious days;
But the fair guerdon when we hope to find,
And think to burst out into sudden blaze,

Comes the blind Fury with the abhorrèd shears,
And slits the thin-spun life. 'But not the praise,'
Phoebus replied, and touched my trembling ears:
'Fame is no plant that grows on mortal soil,
Nor in the glistening foil
Set off to the world, nor in broad rumour lies,
But lives and spreads aloft by those pure eyes
And perfect witness of all-judging Jove;
As he pronounces lastly on each deed,
Of so much fame in heaven expect thy meed.'
   O fountain Arethuse, and thou honoured flood,
Smooth-sliding Mincius, crowned with vocal reeds,
That strain I heard was of a higher mood;
But now my oat proceeds,
And listens to the herald of the sea,
That came in Neptune's plea.
He asked the waves, and asked the felon winds,
What hard mishap hath doomed this gentle swain?
And questioned every gust of rugged wings
That blows from off each beakèd promontory:
They knew not of his story;
And sage Hippotades their answer brings,
That not a blast was from his dungeon strayed;
The air was calm, and on the level brine
Sleek Panope with all her sisters played.
It was that fatal and perfidious bark,
Built in the eclipse, and rigged with curses dark,

That sunk so low that sacred head of thine.
    Next, Camus, reverend sire, went footing slow,
His mantle hairy, and his bonnet sedge,
Inwrought with figures dim, and on the edge
Like to that sanguine flower inscribed with woe.
'Ah! who hath reft,' quoth he, 'my dearest pledge?'
Last came, and last did go,
The pilot of the Galilean lake;
Two massy keys he bore of metals twain
(The golden opes, the iron shuts amain).
He shook his mitred locks, and stern bespake:
'How well could I have spared for thee, young swain,
Enow of such as, for their bellies' sake,
Creep, and intrude, and climb into the fold!
Of other care they little reckoning make
Than how to scramble at the shearers' feast,
And shove away the worthy bidden guest;
Blind mouths! That scarce themselves know how
        to hold
A sheep-hook, or have learned aught else the least
That to the faithful herdman's art belongs!
What recks it them? What need they? They are sped;
And, when they list, their lean and flashy songs
Grate on their scrannel pipes of wretched straw;
The hungry sheep look up, and are not fed,
But, swoll'n with wind and the rank mist they draw,
Rot inwardly, and foul contagion spread;

Besides what the grim wolf with privy paw
Daily devours apace, and nothing said.
But that two-handed engine at the door
Stands ready to smite once, and smite no more.'
    Return, Alpheus; the dread voice is past
That shrunk thy streams; return Sicilian muse,
And call the vales, and bid them hither cast
Their bells and flowerets of a thousand hues.
Ye valleys low, where the mild whispers use
Of shades, and wanton winds, and gushing brooks,
On whose fresh lap the swart star sparely looks,
Throw hither all your quaint enamelled eyes,
That on the green turf suck the honeyed showers,
And purple all the ground with vernal flowers.
Bring the rathe primrose that forsaken dies,
The tufted crow-toe, and pale jessamine,
The white pink, and the pansy freaked with jet,
The glowing violet,
The musk rose, and the well-attired woodbine,
With cowslips wan that hang the pensive head,
And every flower that sad embroidery wears;
Bid amaranthus all his beauty shed,
And daffadillies fill their cups with tears,
To strew the laureate hearse where Lycid lies.
For so, to interpose a little ease,
Let our frail thoughts dally with false surmise.
Ay me! Whilst thee the shores and sounding seas

Wash far away, where'er thy bones are hurled;
Whether beyond the stormy Hebrides,
Where thou perhaps under the whelming tide
Visit'st the bottom of the monstrous world;
Or whether thou, to our moist vows denied,
Sleep'st by the fable of Bellerus old,
Where the great vision of the guarded mount
Looks toward Namancos and Bayona's hold.
Look homeward, angel, now, and melt with ruth;
And, O ye dolphins, waft the hapless youth.

    Weep no more, woeful shepherds, weep no more,
For Lycidas, your sorrow, is not dead,
Sunk though he be beneath the watery floor.
So sinks the day-star in the ocean bed,
And yet anon repairs his drooping head,
And tricks his beams, and with new-spangled ore
Flames in the forehead of the morning sky:
So Lycidas sunk low, but mounted high,
Through the dear might of him that walked the waves,
Where, other groves and other streams along,
With nectar pure his oozy locks he laves,
And hears the unexpressive nuptial song,
In the blest kingdoms meek of joy and love.
There entertain him all the saints above,
In solemn troops, and sweet societies,
That sing, and singing in their glory move,
And wipe the tears for ever from his eyes.

Now, Lycidas, the shepherds weep no more;
Henceforth thou art the genius of the shore,
In thy large recompense, and shalt be good
To all that wander in that perilous flood.

Thus sang the uncouth swain to the oaks and rills,
While the still morn went out with sandals grey;
He touched the tender stops of various quills;
With eager thought warbling his Doric lay:
And now the sun had stretched out all the hills,
And now was dropped into the western bay
At last he rose, and twitched his mantle blue:
To-morrow to fresh woods, and pastures new.

A QUIET SOUL

Thy soul within such silent pomp did keep,
As if humanity were lull'd asleep;
So gentle was thy pilgrimage beneath,
   Time's unheard feet scarce made less noise,
   Of the soft journey which a planet goes:
Life seem'd all calm as its last breath.
   A still tranquillity so hush'd thy breast,
     As if some Halcyon were its guest,
     And there had built her nest;
It hardly now enjoys a greater rest.

TO THE MEMORY OF MR. OLDHAM

Farewell, too little and too lately known,
Whom I began to think and call my own:
For sure our Souls were near alli'd, and thine
Cast in the same poetick mold with mine.
One common Note on either Lyre did strike,
And Knaves and Fools we both abhorr'd alike.
To the same Goal did both our Studies drive:
The last set out the soonest did arrive.
Thus *Nisus* fell upon the slippery place,
Whilst his young Friend perform'd and won the Race.
O early ripe! to thy abundant Store
What could advancing Age have added more?
It might (what Nature never gives the Young)
Have taught the Numbers of thy Native Tongue.
But Satire needs not those, and Wit will shine
Through the harsh Cadence of a rugged Line.

A noble Error, and but seldom made,
When Poets are by too much force betray'd.
Thy gen'rous Fruits, though gather'd ere their prime,
Still shew'd a Quickness; and maturing Time
But mellows what we write to
    the dull Sweets of Rhyme.

Once more, hail, and farewell! farewell, thou young,
But ah! too short, *Marcellus* of our Tongue!
Thy Brows with Ivy and with Laurels bound;
But Fate and gloomy Night encompass thee around.

AT GAUTIER'S GRAVE

To you, gone emblem of man's happiness,
health! Do not think I raise this empty cup
and insane toast to nothingness, because
the non-existent corridor gives hope.
A golden monster suffers on the stem;
your apparition cannot comfort me,
I myself sealed you in your porphyry,
Gautier! The rite is for my hands to dash
their torch against your vault's thick iron gate.
We, who are here simply to celebrate
the absence of the poet, must confess
his sepulchre encloses him entire,
unless the burning glory of his craft,
a window where the light is proud to flash,
answer the mortal sun's pure fire with fire –
ashes to ashes in the common draft!

Marvellous, total, and alone, your boast
was such as false pride trembles to exhale –
that crowd already changing to the pale,
opaque unbeing of its future ghost.
But when fake mourning drapes the blazoned bier,
if one of these dead poets should appear,
serene, deaf even to my sacred verse,
and pass, the guest of his vague shroud, to be

the virgin hero of posterity –
I scorn the lucid horror of a tear.

A vast hole carried by a mass of fog,
the angry wind of words he did not say,
nothingness questions the abolished man:
the dream shrieks, 'Say what the earth was, you,
its shadow! Space has no answer but this toy,
this voice whose clearness falters, "I don't know." '

The master, just by gazing, can reclaim
the restless miracle of paradise.
Once his voice alone was the final frisson
that gave the lily and the rose their name.
Does anything remain of this great claim?
No. Men, forget your narrow faiths, no shade
darkens our métier's artificial fire.

Thinking of you, I call on you: Remain –
Oh lost now in the gardens of this Star –
honour the calm disaster of our earth:
with drunken red words from the loving cup,
a solemn agitation on the air
the crystal gaze of diamonds and rain,
that falls, unfading, on the wilted flower,
the isolation of its sunlit hour.

His tombstone ornaments the garden path –
here is the only true and lasting light,
where the poet's casual, humble gesture ends
the dream that murders his humanity;
today on the great morning of his sleep,
when ancient death is now, as with Gautier,
only the closing of his sacred eyes,
a chance for patience, we too stand and see
this solid sepulchre holds all that hurt:
miserly silence and the massive night.

180   STÉPHANE MALLARMÉ
         TRANS. ROBERT LOWELL

LAMENT FOR THE MAKARIS
Quhen he wes seik

I that in heill wes and glaidnes
Am trublit now with gret seiknes
And feblit with infirmitie;
    Timor Mortis conturbat me.

Our plesance heir is all vane glory,
This fals warld is bot transitory,
The flesche is brukle, the Feynd is sle;
    Timor Mortis conturbat me.

The stait of man dois change and vary,
Now sound, now seik, now blyth, now sary.
Now dans and mirry, now like to dee;
    Timor Mortis conturbat me.

No stait in erd heir standis sickir;
As with the wynd wavis the wickir
So wavis this warldis vanite;
    Timor Mortis conturbat me.

Onto the ded gois all estatis,
Princis, prelotis, and potestatis,
Baith riche and pur of all degre;
    Timor Mortis conturbat me.

He takis the kynchtis in-to feild,
Anarmit vnder helme and scheild;
Wictour he is at all melle;
    Timor Mortis conturbat me.

That strang vnmercifull tyrand
Takis on the moderis breist sowkand
The bab full of benignite;
    Timor Mortis conturbat me.

He takis the campion in the stour,
The capitane closit in the tour,
The lady in bour full of bewte;
    Timor Mortis conturbat me.

He spairis no lord for his piscence,
Na clerk for his intelligence;
His awfull strak may no man fle;
    Timor Mortis conturbat me.

Art magicianis, and astrologgis,
Rethoris, logicians, and theologgis,
Thame helpis no conclusionis sle;
    Timor Mortis conturbat me.

In medecyne the most practicianis,
Lechis, surrigianis, and phisicianis,
Thame-self fra ded may not supple;
    Timor Mortis conturbat me.

I see that makaris amang the laif
Playis heir ther padyanis, syne gois to graif;
Sparit is nocht ther faculte;
    Timor Mortis conturbat me.

He hes done petuously devour
The noble Chaucer, of makaris flouir,
The monk of Bery and Grower all thre;
    Timor Mortis conturbat me.

The gude Syr Hew of Eglintoun,
Ettrik, Heryot, et Wyntoun
He hes tane out of this cuntre;
    Timor Mortis conturbat me.

That scorpioun fell hes done infek
Maister Iohne Clerk and James Afflek
Fra balat making and trigidë;
    Timor Mortis conturbat me.

Holland and Barbour he has berevit;
Allace, that he nought with ws lewit
Schir Mungo Lokert of the Le!
    Timor Mortis conturbat me.

Clerk of Tranent eik he has tane,
That maid the anteris of Gawane;
Schir Gilbert Hay endit has he;
    Timor Mortis conturbat me.

He has Blind Haŕy et Sandy Traill
Slaine with his schot of mortall haill,
Quhilk Patrik Johnistoun myght nought fle;
    Timor Mortis conturbat me.

He hes reft Merseir his endite,
That did in luf so lifly write,
So schort, so quyk, of sentence hie;
    Timor Mortis conturbat me.

He hes tane Roull of Aberdene,
And gentill Roull of Corstorphin;

Two bettir fallowis did no man se;
　　Timor Mortis conturbat me.

In Dunfermelyne he has done rovne
With gude Maister Robert Henrisoun;
Schir Iohne the Ros enbrast hes he;
　　Timor Mortis conturbat me.

And he has now tane, last of aw,
Gud gentill Stobo and Quintyne Schaw,
Of quham all wichtis hes pete;
　　Timor Mortis conturbat me.

Gud Maister Walter Kennedy
In poynt of dede lyis veraly;
Gret reuth it wer that so suld be;
　　Timor Mortis conturbat me.

Sen he has all my brether tane,
He will naught lat me lif alane;
On forse I man his nyxt pray be;
　　Timor Mortis conturbat me.

Sen for the deid remeid is non,
Best is that we for deid dispone,
Eftir our deid that lif may we;
　　Timor Mortis conturbat me.

WILLIAM DUNBAR   185

I TRAVELLED AMONG
UNKNOWN MEN

I travelled among unknown men,
   In lands beyond the sea;
Nor, England! Did I know till then
   What love I bore to thee.

'Tis past, that melancholy dream!
   Nor will I quit thy shore
A second time; for still I seem
   To love thee more and more.

Among thy mountains did I feel
   The joy of my desire;
And she I cherished turned her wheel
   Beside an English fire.

Thy mornings showed, thy nights concealed,
   The bowers where Lucy played;
And thine too is the last green field
   That Lucy's eyes surveyed.

FIELD DAY

The old farmer, nearing death, asked
To be carried outside and set down
Where he could see a certain field
'And then I will cry my heart out,' he said.

It troubles me, thinking about that man;
What shape was the field of his crying
In Donegal?

I remember a small field in Down, a field
Within fields, shaped like a triangle.
I could have stood there and looked at it
All day long.

And I remember crossing the frontier between
France and Spain at a forbidden point, and seeing
A small triangular field in Spain,
And stopping

Or walking in Ireland down any rutted by-road
To where it hit the highway, there was always
At this turning-point and abutment
A still centre, a V-shape of grass

Untouched by cornering traffic,
Where country lads larked at night.

I think I know what the shape of the field was
That made the old man weep.

DAVID'S EPITAPH ON JONATHAN

Here lyes the fairest Flowre, that stood
In Isr'el's Garden; now, in Blood;
Which, Death to make her Girland gay,
Hath cropt, against her Triumph Day:
Here, here lies Hee, whose Actions pen'd
The perfect Copie of a Frend,
Whose milk-white Vellam did incurre
No least suspition of a Blurre:
Here lyes th'example of a Brother,
Not to bee follow'd by another;
The faire-indented Counter-part
Of David's Joy, of David's Heart:
Rest then; For ever, rest alone;
Thy Ashes can be touch'd by none,
Till Death hath pickt out such another:
Here lyes a Flow'r, a Friend, a Brother.

TO HIS LOVE

He's gone, and all our plans
   Are useless indeed.
We'll walk no more on Cotswold
   Where the sheep feed
   Quietly and take no heed.

His body that was so quick
   Is not as you
Knew it, on Severn river
   Under the blue
   Driving our small boat through.

You would not know him now . . .
   But still he died
Nobly, so cover him over
   With violets of pride
   Purple from Severn side.

Cover him, cover him soon!
   And with thick-set
Masses of memoried flowers –
   Hide that red wet
   Thing I must somehow forget.

FLETCHER'S LAMENT FOR HIS FRIEND

Come, sorrow, come! bring all thy cries,
All thy laments, and all thy weeping eyes!
Burn out, you living monuments of woe!
Sad, sullen griefs, now rise and overflow!
   Virtue is dead;
   Oh! cruel fate!
   All youth is fled;
   All our laments too late.
Oh, noble youth, to thy ne'er dying name,
Oh, happy youth, to thy still growing fame,
To thy long peace in earth, this sacred knell
Our last loves ring – farewell, farewell, farewell!
Go, happy soul, to thy eternal birth!
And press his body lightly, gentle Earth.

SHE

I think the dead are tender. Shall we kiss? –
My lady laughs, delighting in what is.
If she but sighs, a bird puts out its tongue.
She makes space lonely with a lovely song.
She lilts a low soft language, and I hear
Down long sea-chambers of the inner ear.

We sing together; we sing mouth to mouth.
The garden is a river flowing south.
She cries out loud the soul's own secret joy;
She dances, and the ground bears her away.
She knows the speech of light, and makes it plain
A lively thing can come to life again.

I feel her presence in the common day,
In that slow dark that widens every eye.
She moves as water moves, and comes to me,
Stayed by what was, and pulled by what would be.

THE VOICE

Woman much missed, how you call to me, call to me,
Saying that now you are not as you were
When you had changed
   from the one who was all to me,
But as at first, when our day was fair.

Can it be you that I hear? Let me view you, then,
Standing as when I drew near to the town
Where you would wait for me: yes, as I knew you then,
Even to the original air-blue gown!

Or is it only the breeze, in its listlessness
Travelling across the wet mead to me here,
You being ever dissolved to wan wistlessness,
Heard no more again far or near?

      Thus I; faltering forward,
      Leaves around me falling,
Wind oozing thin through the thorn from norward,
      And the woman calling.

LONG DISTANCE

I

Your bed's got two wrong sides. Your life's all grouse.
I let your phone-call take its dismal course:

Ah can't stand it no more, this empty house!

Carrots choke us wi'out your mam's white sauce!

Them sweets you brought me, you can have 'em back.
Ah'm diabetic now. Got all the facts.
(The diabetes comes hard on the track
of two coronaries and cataracts.)

Ah've allus liked things sweet! But now ah push
food down mi throat! Ah'd sooner do wi'out.
And t'only reason now for beer's to flush
(so t'dietician said) mi kidneys out.

When I come round, they'll be laid out, the sweets,
Lifesavers, my father's New World treats,
still in the big brown bag, and only bought
rushing through JFK as a last thought.

II

Though my mother was already two years dead
Dad kept her slippers warming by the gas,
put hot water bottles her side of the bed
and still went to renew her transport pass.

You couldn't just drop in. You had to phone.
He'd put you off an hour to give him time
to clear away her things and look alone
as though his still raw love were such a crime.

He couldn't risk my blight of disbelief
though sure that very soon he'd hear her key
scrape in the rusted lock and end his grief.
He *knew* she'd just popped out to get the tea.

I believe life ends with death, and that is all.
You haven't both gone shopping; just the same,
in my new black leather phone book there's your name
and the disconnected number I still call.

TONY HARRISON   195

A SLUMBER DID MY SPIRIT SEAL

A slumber did my spirit seal;
   I had no human fears:
She seemed a thing that could not feel
   The touch of earthly years.

No motion has she now, no force;
   She neither hears nor sees;
Rolled round in earth's diurnal course,
   With rocks, and stones, and trees.

PROPERTIUS, ELEGIES II, 28

When thou must home to shades of under ground,
And there ariv'd, a newe admired guest,
The beauteous spirits do ingirt thee round,
White Iope, blith Hellen, and the rest,
To heare the stories of thy finisht love
From that smoothe toong whose musicke hell
     can move;

Then wilt thou speake of banqueting delights,
Of masks and revels which sweete youth did make,
Of Turnies and great challenges of knights,
And all these triumphes for thy beauties sake:
When thou hast told these honours done to thee,
Then tell, O tell, how thou didst murther me.

TO LIZBIE BROWNE

I

Dear Lizbie Browne,
Where are you now?
In sun, in rain? –
Or is your brow
Past joy, past pain,
Dear Lizbie Browne?

II

Sweet Lizbie Browne,
How you could smile,
How you could sing! –
How archly wile
In glance-giving,
Sweet Lizbie Browne!

III

And, Lizbie Browne,
Who else had hair
Bay-red as yours,
Or flesh so fair
Bred out of doors,
Sweet Lizbie Browne?

IV

When, Lizbie Browne,
You had just begun
To be endeared
By stealth to one,
You disappeared
My Lizbie Browne!

V

Ay, Lizbie Browne,
So swift your life,
And mine so slow,
You were a wife
Ere I could show
Love, Lizbie Browne.

VI

Still, Lizbie Browne,
You won, they said,
The best of men
When you were wed ...
Where went you then,
O Lizbie Browne?

VII

Dear Lizbie Browne,
I should have thought,
'Girls ripen fast,'
And coaxed and caught
You ere you passed,
Dear Lizbie Browne!

VIII

But, Lizbie Browne,
I let you slip;
Shaped not a sign;
Touched never your lip
With lip of mine,
Lost Lizbie Browne!

IX

So, Lizbie Browne,
When on a day
Men speak of me
As not, you'll say,
'And who was he?' –
Yes, Lizbie Browne!

AN EXCHANGE OF FEELINGS

In the old park, deserted in the frost,
A while ago two shapes came drifting past.

Their eyes have died, their lips become so weak
That you can hardly hear a word they speak.

In the old park, deserted in the frost,
A ghost was reminiscing to a ghost.

– Can you recall our ecstasy of long ago?
– Why stir the memory? Why do you want to know?

– Does your heart beat at just my name, as ever?
Do you still see my spirit in your dreams? – No. Never.

– O lovely days of speechless happiness
When our mouths met! – Speechless? Perhaps it was.

– How blue the sky was and what hopes we had!
– Hope ran away to the black sky, defeated.

So they walk on in the self-seeding grass
With only night to hear them as they pass.

PAUL VERLAINE   201
TRANS. ALISTAIR ELLIOT

From ANACTORIA

Yea, thou shalt be forgotten like spilt wine,
Except these kisses of my lips on thine
Brand them with immortality; but me –
Men shall not see bright fire nor hear the sea,
Nor mix their hearts with music, nor behold
Cast forth of heaven, with feet of awful gold
And plumeless wings that make the bright air blind,
Lightning, with thunder for a hound behind
Hunting through fields unfurrowed and unsown,
But in the light and laughter, in the moan
And music, and in grasp of lip and hand
And shudder of water that makes felt on land
The immeasurable tremor of all the sea,
Memories shall mix and metaphors of me.

THE OLD GOWN

I have seen her in gowns the brightest,
    Of azure, green, and red,
And in the simplest, whitest,
    Muslined from heel to head;
I have watched her walking, riding,
    Shade-flecked by a leafy tree,
Or in fixed thought abiding
    By the foam-fingered sea.

In woodlands I have known her,
    When boughs were mourning loud,
In the rain-reek she has shown her
    Wild-haired and watery-browed.
And once or twice she has cast me
    As she pomped along the street
Court-clad, ere quite she had passed me,
    A glance from her chariot-seat,

But in my memoried passion
    For evermore stands she
In the gown of fading fashion
    She wore that night when we,
Doomed long to part, assembled
    In the snug small room; yea, when
She sang with lips that trembled,
    'Shall I see his face again?'

THOMAS HARDY

FUNERAL BLUES

Stop all the clocks, cut off the telephone,
Prevent the dog from barking with a juicy bone,
Silence the pianos and with muffled drum
Bring out the coffin, let the mourners come.

Let aeroplanes circle moaning overhead
Scribbling on the sky the message He Is Dead,
Put crêpe bows round the white necks of the public
    doves,
Let the traffic policemen wear black cotton gloves.

He was my North, my South, my East and West,
My working week and my Sunday rest,
My noon, my midnight, my talk, my song;
I thought that love would last for ever: I was wrong.

The stars are not wanted now: put out every one;
Pack up the moon and dismantle the sun;
Pour away the ocean and sweep up the wood;
For nothing now can ever come to any good.

TO HIS DEAD BODY

When roaring gloom surged inward and you cried,
Groping for friendly hands, and clutched, and died,
Like racing smoke, swift from your lolling head
Phantoms of thought and memory thinned and fled.

Yet, though my dreams that throng the darkened stair
Can bring me no report of how you fare,
Safe quit of wars, I speed you on your way
Up lonely, glimmering fields to find new day,
Slow-rising, saintless, confident and kind –
Dear, red-faced father God who lit your mind.

THE SILENT ONE

Who died on the wires, and hung there, one of two –
Who for his hours of life had chattered through
Infinite lovely chatter of Bucks accent:
Yet faced unbroken wires; stepped over, and went
A noble fool, faithful to his stripes – and ended.
But I weak, hungry, and willing only for the chance
Of line – to fight in the line, lay down under unbroken
Wires, and saw the flashes and kept unshaken,
Till the politest voice – a finicking accent, said:
'Do you think you might crawl through there: there's a
     hole.'
Darkness, shot at: I smiled, as politely replied –
'I'm afraid not, Sir.' There was no hole no way to be
     seen
Nothing but chance of death, after tearing of clothes.
Kept flat, and watched the darkness, hearing bullets
     whizzing –
And thought of music – and swore deep heart's deep
     oaths
(Polite to God) and retreated and came on again,
Again retreated – and a second time faced the screen.

ANTHEM FOR DOOMED YOUTH

What passing-bells for these who die as cattle?
    – Only the monstrous anger of the guns.
    Only the stuttering rifles' rapid rattle
Can patter out their hasty orisons.
No mockeries now for them; no prayers nor bells;
    Nor any voice of mourning save the choirs, –
The shrill, demented choirs of wailing shells;
    And bugles calling for them from sad shires.

What candles may be held to speed them all?
    Not in the hands of boys but in their eyes
Shall shine the holy glimmers of goodbyes.
    The pallor of girls' brows shall be their pall;
Their flowers the tenderness of patient minds,
And each slow dusk a drawing-down of blinds.

WILFRED OWEN   207

THE TOMBSTONE-MAKER

He primmed his loose red mouth and leaned his head
Against a sorrowing angel's breast, and said:
'You'd think so much bereavement would have made
'Unusual big demands upon my trade.
'The War comes cruel hard on some poor folk;
'Unless the fighting stops I'll soon be broke.'

He eyed the Cemetery across the road.
'There's scores of bodies out abroad, this while,
'That should be here by rights. They little know'd
'How they'd get buried in such wretched style.'

I told him with a sympathetic grin,
That Germans boil dead soldiers down for fat;
And he was horrified. 'What shameful sin!
'O sir, that Christian souls should come to that!'

IN MEMORIAM (LXVII)

When on my bed the moonlight falls,
    I know that in thy place of rest
    By that broad water of the west,
There comes a glory on the walls:

Thy marble bright in dark appears,
    As slowly steals a silver flame
    Along the letters of thy name,
And o'er the number of thy years.

The mystic glory swims away;
    From off my bed the moonlight dies;
    And closing eaves of wearied eyes
I sleep till dusk is dipt in gray:

And then I know the mist is drawn
    A lucid veil from coast to coast,
    And in the dark church like a ghost
Thy tablet glimmers to the dawn.

ALFRED, LORD TENNYSON

AFTER DEATH

The curtains were half drawn, the floor was swept
    And strewn with rushes, rosemary and may
Lay thick upon the bed on which I lay,
Where through the lattice ivy-shadows crept.
He leaned above me, thinking that I slept
    And could not hear him; but I heard him say,
    'Poor child, poor child': and as he turned away
Came a deep silence, and I knew he wept.
He did not touch the shroud, or raise the fold
    That hid my face, or take my hand in his,
        Or ruffle the smooth pillows for my head:
        He did not love me living; but once dead
    He pitied me; and very sweet it is
To know he still is warm though I am cold.

THE SURVIVOR
to B.V.

Dopo di allora, ad ora incerta,
Since then, at an uncertain hour,
That agony returns:
And till my ghastly tale is told,
This heart within me burns.

Once more he sees his companions' faces
Livid in the first faint light,
Gray with cement dust,
Nebulous in the mist,
Tinged with death in their uneasy sleep.
At night, under the heavy burden
Of their dreams, their jaws move,
Chewing a nonexistent turnip.
'Stand back, leave me alone, submerged people,
Go away. I haven't dispossessed anyone,
Haven't usurped anyone's bread.
No one died in my place. No one.
Go back into your mist.
It's not my fault if I live and breathe,
Eat, drink, sleep and put on clothes.'

TRANS. RUTH FELDMAN AND BRIAN SWANN

THE PARDON

My dog lay dead five days without a grave
In the thick of summer, hid in a clump of pine
And a jungle of grass and honeysuckle-vine.
I who had loved him while he kept alive

Went only close enough to where he was
To sniff the heavy honeysuckle-smell
Twined with another odor heavier still
And hear the flies' intolerable buzz.

Well, I was ten and very much afraid.
In my kind world the dead were out of range
And I could not forgive the sad or strange
In beast or man. My father took the spade

And buried him. Last night I saw the grass
Slowly divide (it was the same scene
But now it glowed a fierce and mortal green)
And saw the dog emerging. I confess

I felt afraid again, but still he came
In the carnal sun, clothed in a hymn of flies,
And death was breeding in his lively eyes.
I started in to cry and call his name,

Asking forgiveness of his tongueless head.
... I dreamt the past was never past redeeming:
But whether this was false or honest dreaming
I beg death's pardon now. And mourn the dead.

AT A DOG'S GRAVE

I

Good night, we say, when comes the time to win
The daily death divine that shuts up sight,
Sleep, that assures for all who dwell therein
   Good night.

The shadow shed round those we love shines bright
As love's own face, when death, sleep's gentler twin,
From them divides us even as night from light.

Shall friends born lower in life, though pure of sin,
Though clothed with love and faith to usward plight,
Perish and pass unbidden of us, their kin,
   Good night?

II

To die a dog's death once was held for shame.
Not all men so beloved and mourned shall lie
As many of these, whose time untimely came
   To die.

His years were full: his years were joyous: why
Must love be sorrow, when his gracious name
Recalls his lovely life of limb and eye?

If aught of blameless life on earth may claim
Life higher than death, though death's dark wave
    rise high,
Such life as this among us never came
  To die.

III

White violets, there by hands more sweet than they
Planted, shall sweeten April's flowerful air
About a grave that shows to night and day
  White violets there.

A child's light hands, whose touch makes flowers
    more fair,
Keep fair as these for many a March and May
The light of days that are because they were.

It shall not like a blossom pass away;
It broods and brightens with the days that bear
Fresh fruits of love, but leave, as love might pray,
  White violets there.

PRAISE OF A COLLIE

She was a small dog, neat and fluid –
Even her conversation was tiny:
She greeted you with *bow*, never *bow-wow*.

Her sons stood monumentally over her
But did what she told them. Each grew grizzled
Till it seemed he was his own mother's grandfather.

Once, gathering sheep on a showery day,
I remarked how dry she was. Pollóchan said, 'Ah,
It would take a very accurate drop to hit Lassie.'

And her tact – and tactics! When the sheep bolted
In an unforeseen direction, over the skyline
Came – who but Lassie, and not even panting.

She sailed in the dinghy like a proper sea-dog.
Where's a burn? – she's first on the other side.
She flowed through fences like a piece of black wind.

But suddenly she was old and sick and crippled ...
I grieved for Pollóchan when he took her for a stroll
And put his gun to the back of her head.

From THE ODYSSEY OF HOMER, BOOK XVII

Such speech they changed: when in the yard there lay
A dog, call'd Argus, which, before his way
Assumed for Ilion, Ulysses bred,
Yet stood his pleasure then in little stead,
As being too young, but, growing to his grace,
Young men made choice of him for every chace,
Or of their wild goats, of their hares, or harts.
But, his king gone, and he, now past his parts,
Lay all abjectly on the stable's store,
Before the ox-stall, and mules' stable door,
To keep the clothes cast from the peasants' hands,
While they laid compass on Ulysses' lands,
The dog, with ticks (unlook'd to) overgrown.
But by this dog no sooner seen but known
Was wise Ulysses, who new enter'd there,
Up went his dog's laid ears, and, coming near,
Up he himself rose, fawn'd, and wagg'd his stern,
Couch'd close his ears, and lay so; nor discern
Could evermore his dear-loved lord again.
Ulysses saw it, nor had power t' abstain
From shedding tears; which (far-off seeing his swain)
He dried from his sight clean; to whom he thus
His grief dissembled: "Tis miraculous,
That such a dog as this should have his lair

On such a dunghill, for his form is fair.
And yet, I know not, if there were in him
Good pace, or parts, for all his goodly limb;
Or he lived empty of those inward things,
As are those trencher-beagles tending kings,
Whom for their pleasure's, or their glory's, sake,
Or fashion, they into their favours take.'
    'This dog,' said he, 'was servant to one dead
A huge time since. But if he bore his head,
For form and quality, of such a height,
As when Ulysses, bound for th'Ilion fight,
Or quickly after, left him, your rapt eyes
Would then admire to see him use his thighs
In strength and swiftness. He would nothing fly,
Nor anything let 'scape. If once his eye
Seized any wild beast, he knew straight his scent;
Go where he would, away with him he went.
Nor was there ever any savage stood
Amongst the thickets of the deepest wood
Long time before him, but he pull'd him down;
As well by that true hunting to be shown
In such vast coverts, as for speed of pace
In any open lawn. For in deep chace
He was a passing wise and well-nosed hound.
And yet is all this good in him uncrown'd
With any grace here now, nor he more fed
Than any errant cur. His king is dead,

Far from his country; and his servants are
So negligent they lend his hound no care.
Where masters rule not, but let men alone,
You never there see honest service done.
That man's half virtue Jove takes quite away,
That once is sun-burnt with the servile day.'

ODE ON THE DEATH OF A FAVOURITE CAT, DROWNED IN A TUB OF GOLD FISHES

'Twas on a lofty vase's side,
Where China's gayest art had dyed
   The azure flowers that blow;
Demurest of the tabby kind,
The pensive Selima reclined,
   Gazed on the lake below.

Her conscious tail her joy declared;
The fair round face, the snowy beard,
   The velvet of her paws,
Her coat, that with the tortoise vies,
Her ears of jet and emerald eyes,
   She saw; and purred applause.

Still had she gazed; but 'midst the tide
Two angel forms were seen to glide,
   The Genii of the stream:
Their scaly armour's Tyrian hue
Thro' richest purple to the view
   Betray'd a golden gleam.

The hapless Nymph with wonder saw:
A whisker first and then a claw,

With many an ardent wish,
She stretch'd in vain to reach the prize.
What female heart can gold despise?
    What Cat's averse to fish?

Presumptuous Maid! with looks intent
Again she stretch'd, again she bent,
    Nor knew the gulf between.
(Malignant Fate sat by, and smiled.)
The slipp'ry verge her feet beguiled,
    She tumbled headlong in.

Eight times emerging from the flood
She mew'd to every wat'ry god,
    Some speedy aid to send.
No Dolphin came, no Nereid stirr'd:
No cruel *Tom* nor *Susan* heard.
    A Fav'rite has no friend!

From hence, ye Beauties undeceiv'd,
Know, one false step is ne'er retriev'd,
    And be with caution bold.
Not all that tempts your wand'ring eyes
And heedless hearts, is lawful prize;
    Nor all that glisters, gold.

THOMAS GRAY   221

ON THE DEATH OF A MONKEY

Here *Busy* and yet *Innocent* lyes Dead,
    Two things, that seldom meet:
No Plots nor Stratagems disturb'd his head,
    Or's merry Soul did fret:
He shew'd like Superannuated *Peer*,
Grave was his look, and *Politick* his Air;
    And he for *Nothing* too spent all his care.

But that he died of Discontent, 'tis fear'd,
    Head of the *Monkey* Rout;
To see so many Brother *Apes* preferr'd,
    And he himself left out:
On all below he did his Anger show'r,
Fit for a Court did all above adore,
H'had *Shows* of Reason, and few *Men* have more.

PARTRIDGE

Never, my partridge, O patient heart,
Were you to see your hills again.
And never now will you wake up
In your elegant wicker coop,
Shake as the fat-eyed day comes on,
And freckle your wings with the dawn.
The greedy cat has got your head,
I've taken what's left from her teeth
And hidden you well from her claws.
Small bodies should not lie so deep.
May the dust be light on your grave.

A DEAD MOLE

Strong-shouldered mole,
That so much lived below the ground,
Dug, fought and loved, hunted and fed,
For you to raise a mound
Was as for us to make a hole;
What wonder now that being dead
Your body lies here stout and square
Buried within the blue vault of the air?

EPITAPH ON A DORMOUSE,
REALLY WRITTEN BY
A LITTLE BOY

In Paper Case,
Hard by this Place,
Dead a poor Dormouse lies;
And soon or late,
Summon'd by Fate,
Each Prince, each Monarch dies.

Ye Sons of Verse,
While I rehearse,
Attend instructive Rhyme;
Nor Sins had *Dor*,
To answer for,
Repent of yours in Time.

ANON.   225

CARMEN III

Cupids and Graces, mourn with me --
Men, too, of sensibility:
Gone is my darling's sparrow, gone
The sparrow that she doted on.

She loved him more than her own eyes,
For he, sweet thing, would recognise
His mistress as a maid her mother,
Nor leave her lap for any other,
But hither alight and thither spring,
In her sole service chirruping.

And now the shadow-glimmering track
He goes, whence none – they say – come back.

Ill tide you, dark and evil power,
You, that all prettiness devour –
So pretty a sparrow have you torn
Away, O cruel, for us to mourn.
Poor bird, for you my darling cries,
All red, and big with tears, her eyes.

226   CATULLUS
        TRANS. ANON.

EPITAPH ON A HARE

Here lies, whom hound did ne'er pursue,
 Nor swifter greyhound follow,
Whose foot ne'er tainted morning dew,
 Nor ear heard huntsman's 'hallo',

Old Tiney, surliest of his kind,
 Who, nursed with tender care,
And to domestic bounds confined,
 Was still a wild jack-hare.

Though duly from my hand he took
 His pittance ev'ry night,
He did it with a jealous look,
 And, when he could, would bite.

His diet was of wheaten bread,
 And milk, and oats, and straw,
Thistles, or lettuces instead,
 With sand to scour his maw.

On twigs of hawthorn he regaled,
 On pippins' russet peel;
And, when his juicy salads failed,
 Sliced carrot pleased him well.

A Turkey carpet was his lawn,
  Whereon he loved to bound,
To skip and gambol like a fawn,
  And swing his rump around.

His frisking was at evening hours,
  For then he lost his fear;
But most before approaching show'rs,
  Or when a storm drew near.

Eight years and five round-rolling moons
  He thus saw steal away,
Dozing out all his idle noons,
  And ev'ry night at play.

I kept him for his humour's sake,
  For he would oft beguile
My heart of thoughts that made it ache,
  And force me to a smile.

But now, beneath this walnut-shade
  He finds his long, last home,
And waits in snug concealment laid,
  Till gentler Puss shall come.

He, still more agèd, feels the shocks
    From which no care can save,
And, partner once of Tiney's box,
    Must soon partake his grave.

AN EPITAPH UPON THE CELEBRATED CLAUDY PHILIPS, MUSICIAN, WHO DIED VERY POOR

Philips, whose touch harmonious could remove
The pangs of guilty pow'r, and hapless love,
Rest here, distress'd by poverty no more,
Here find that calm, thou gav'st so oft before.
Sleep, undisturb'd, within this peaceful shrine,
Till angels wake thee, with a note like thine.

AN EPITAPH ON M. H.

In this cold *Monument* lies one,
That I know who has lain upon,
The happier *He:* her Sight would charm,
And Touch have kept *King David* warm.
Lovely, as is the dawning *East*,
Was this Marble's frozen *Guest*;
As soft, and Snowy, as that Down
Adorns the *Blow-balls* frizled Crown;
As straight and slender as the *Crest*,
Or *Antlet* of the one-beam'd Beast;
Pleasant as th'odorous *Month* of *May*:
As glorious, and as light as *Day*.

   Whom I admir'd, as soon as knew,
And now her Memory pursue
With such a superstitious Lust,
That I could fumble with her Dust.

   She all Perfections had, and more,
Tempting, as if design'd a *Whore*,
For so she was; and since there are
Such, I could wish them all as fair.

   Pretty she was, and young, and wise,
And in her Calling so precise,

That Industry had made her prove
The sucking *School-Mistress* of *Love*:
And *Death*, ambitious to become
Her *Pupil*, left his Ghastly home,
And, seeing how we us'd her here,
The raw-bon'd *Rascal* ravisht her.

Who, pretty *Soul*, resign'd her Breath,
To seek new Letchery in Death.

MEMORIAL TABLET
(GREAT WAR)

Squire nagged and bullied till I went to fight,
(Under Lord Derby's Scheme). I died in hell –
(They called it Passchendaele). My wound was slight,
And I was hobbling back; and then a shell
Burst slick upon the duck-boards: so I fell
Into the bottomless mud, and lost the light.

At sermon-time, while Squire is in his pew,
He gives my gilded name a thoughtful stare:
For, though low down upon the list, I'm there;
'In proud and glorious memory' . . . that's my due.
Two bleeding years I fought in France, for Squire:
I suffered anguish that he's never guessed.
Once I came home on leave: and then went west . . .
What greater glory could a man desire?

SIEGFRIED SASSOON   233

EPITAPH ON THE DUKE
OF GRAFTON

    Here
  Lyes a Peer
  Beneath this Place
  Stil'd his Grace
  The Duke of Grafton,
A Blade as fine, as e're had Haft on.
Markt with a Garter and a Star
Forg'd out, and ground for War;
  Of Mettle true
  As ever drew,
  Or made a Pass
  At Lad or Lass.
This Valiant Son of Mars
  Ne're hung an Arse
  With Sword or Tarse,
  Nor turn'd his Tail,
  Tho' Shots like Hail
  Flew about his Ears
  With Spikes and Spears
So Thick, they'd hide the Sun.
  He boldly forc'd his Way
  Leading the Van
More like the Devil than a Man:
For why, he valu'd not a Fart a Gun.

He ne're wou'd Dread
Bullets of Lead,
Nor Cannon Ball
Nothing at all;
But a Bullet of Cork
Soon did his Work
Unhappy Pellet
With Greif I tell it
For with one Blow thou hast Undone
Great Cæsar's Son:
A Soldier foil'd
A Statesman Spoil'd.
God Rot him
That shot him
For a Son of a Whore,
Ile say no more,
But Here lyes Henry Duke of Grafton.

EPITAPH ON A TOMB NEAR ROME

Squander for me no scent of myrrh
Spread no myrtle on my tomb
Kindle me no burning pyre
What's the use of such waste

My dust will turn to clay & mire
For all your purple, flowing wine
Give the living their desire
Dead men conspicuously have no taste

ANON.

TRANS. FRANZ KUENSTLER

DEAR TO ME IS SLEEP

Dear to me is sleep: still more, being made of stone.
While pain and guilt still linger here below,
Blindness and numbness – these please me alone;
Then do not wake me, keep your voices low.

AN EPITAPH FOR A GODLY MAN'S TOMB

Here lies a piece of Christ, a Star in Dust;
A Vein of Gold, a China Dish that must
Be us'd in Heav'n, when God shall Feast the Just.

ROBERT WILDE

'TWAS MY ONE GLORY

'Twas my one Glory –
Let it be
Remembered
I was owned of Thee –

R.M.R.

4 December 1875–29 December 1926

ROSE, OH THE PURE CONTRADICTION,
DELIGHT, OF BEING NO ONE'S SLEEP
UNDER SO MANY LIDS.

ACKNOWLEDGMENTS

Thanks are due to the following copyright holders for their permission to reprint:

AL-MA'ARRI, ABU AL-ALA: 'The soul driven from the body' and 'Needles have stitched a death shroud' from *Birds Through a Ceiling of Alabaster: Three Abbasid Poets*, tr. Abdullah al-Udhari and George Wightman (Penguin Classics, 1975) copyright © G. B. H. Wightman and A. Y. al-Udhari, 1975. Reproduced by permission of Penguin Books Ltd. ANNENSKY, INNOKENTY: 'Black Spring' from *Imitations* by Robert Lowell. Copyright © 1959 by Robert Lowell. Copyright renewed © 1987 by Harriet, Sheridan, and Caroline Lowell. Reprinted by permission of Farrar, Straus & Giroux, Inc. and Faber and Faber Ltd. ATTAR: 'The Sufi who thought he had left the world' from *The Conference of the Birds* by Farid ud-din Attar, tr. Afkham Darbandi and Dick Davis (Penguin Classics, 1984) copyright © Afkham Darbandi and Dick Davis, 1984. Reproduced by permission of Penguin Books Ltd. AUDEN, W. H.: 'An Island Cemetery', 'At the Grave of Henry James' and 'Twelve Songs IX' from *W. H. Auden: Collected Poems*, ed. Edward Mendelson. Respectively, copyright © 1960, 1940 and renewed 1968 by W. H. Auden, 1941 and renewed 1969 by W. H. Auden.

Sheridan, and Caroline Lowell. Reprinted by permission of Farrar, Straus & Giroux, Inc. and Faber and Faber Ltd. OSIP MANDELSTAM: 'To Praise a Dead Woman' from *The Voronezh Notebooks*, tr. Richard and Elizabeth McKane, Bloodaxe Books, 1996. MENG CHIAO: 'Lament for Lu Yin', tr. Stephen Owen. From *Sunflower Splendour*. Reprinted by permission. MICHELANGELO BUONARROTI: 'To Luigi del Riccio after the Death of Cecchino Bracci' and 'Dear to me is sleep' from *The Sonnets of Michelangelo*, Carcanet, tr. Elizabeth Jennings. Reprinted by permission of David Higham Associates. CZESLAW MILOSZ: 'On Parting with My Wife, Janina' and 'With Her' from *The Collected Poems 1931–1987* (Viking, 1988) by Czeslaw Milosz, tr. the Author and Robert Hass. Copyright © 1988 by Czeslaw Milosz Royalties, Inc. Reprinted by permission of The Ecco Press and Penguin Books Ltd. EDWIN MUIR: 'The Child Dying' from *Collected Poems* by Edwin Muir. Copyright © 1960 by Willa Muir. Reprinted by permission of Oxford University Press, Inc. and Faber and Faber Ltd. WILFRED OWEN: 'Anthem for Doomed Youth' from *The Collected Poems of Wilfred Owen*. Copyright © 1963 by Chatto and Windus. Reprinted by permission of New Directions Publishing Corp., the Estate of Wilfred Owen and Chatto and Windus. RAINER MARIA RILKE: 'The Poet's Death' and 'Roman Sarcophagi' from *New Poems*, tr.

243

INDEX OF AUTHORS